NAMING NATURE

NAMING NATURE

A Cabinet of Natural
Curiosities for Word Lovers

T. A. BARRON

RIVERSIDE PRESS

CONTENTS

INTRODUCTION
This Living Circle:
An Invitation from the Author
10

CHAPTER 1
High Fliers
16

RESPLENDENT QUETZAL • MEADOWLARK
HALCYON BIRD • HUMMINGBIRD • ALBATROSS
BOWERBIRD • GOLDCREST • HUET-HUET
SCREAMING PIHA • MERLIN • PREDICTED ANTWREN
WATER OUZEL • PILMAIQUEN • TIMBERDOODLE

AN ENCOUNTER WITH SANDHILL CRANES

CHAPTER 2
Wonders of the Water
54

GOBLIN SHARK • LEAFY SEA DRAGON
NUDIBRANCH • AMAZON PINK DOLPHIN
MOON JELLY • RED-LIPPED BATFISH • HUMPBACK WHALE
HUMUHUMUNUKUNUKUAPUA'A • ORGAN PIPE CORAL
SEA BUTTERFLY • SARCASTIC FRINGEHEAD

AN ENCOUNTER WITH A WHALE

CHAPTER 3

Roots and Rainbows

82

DRAGON'S MOUTH ORCHID • RAINBOW EUCALYPTUS
BIRD OF PARADISE FLOWER • FOXGLOVE • MOONFLOWER
SEMPERVIRENS • VENUS FLYTRAP • ALERCE • ELEPHANT HEAD
FLOWER • BABY TOOTH MOSS • MAIDENHAIR FERN
GRASS OF PARNASSUS • KISS-ME-OVER-THE-GARDEN-GATE

AN ENCOUNTER WITH AN ANCIENT REDWOOD TREE

CHAPTER 4

Inspiring Insects

116

DRAGONFLY • MADAGASCAN SUNSET MOTH
NAMIB DESERT BEETLE • MORPHO BUTTERFLY
FIREFLY • LUNA MOTH • PRAYING MANTIS

AN ENCOUNTER WITH A LUNA MOTH

CHAPTER 5

Invisible Neighbours

140

GHOST CRAB • UNICORN OF THE SEA
DIATOM • METHUSELAH'S BEARD LICHEN
SNOW LEOPARD • TRUFFLE • YETI

AN ENCOUNTER WITH A SNOW LEOPARD

CHAPTER 6

Strange Swimmers and Slitherers

164

ELECTRIC EEL • PINOCCHIO FROG
MARINE IGUANA • HELLBENDER
EMERALD TREE BOA • POISON DART FROG
AXOLOTL • PUMPKIN TOADLET

AN ENCOUNTER WITH A MARINE IGUANA

CHAPTER 7

Magnificent Mammals

188

SPIRIT BEAR • DUGONG • ELEPHANT • PLATYPUS
CHIMPANZEE • KOALA • CARIBOU • PINK FAIRY ARMADILLO
GIRAFFE • EMPEROR TAMARIN • RACCOON

AN ENCOUNTER WITH A MOUNTAIN GORILLA

CHAPTER 8

Creatures Fabulous and Frightening

226

BIOLUMINESCENT ALGAE • GOOSENECK BARNACLE
MANTIS SHRIMP • WUNDERPUS OCTOPUS
ELEGANT SUNBURST LICHEN • BY-THE-WIND SAILOR
GOLIATH BIRD-EATING TARANTULA • VAMPIRE SQUID

AN ENCOUNTER WITH A GIANT PACIFIC OCTOPUS

INDEX   251
CREDITS   254
ACKNOWLEDGEMENTS   255

Those who contemplate the beauty of the earth find reserves of strength that will endure as long as life lasts.

RACHEL CARSON, *THE SENSE OF WONDER*

INTRODUCTION

This Living Circle

AN INVITATION FROM THE AUTHOR

Early in the darkness before dawn, I often lie awake, listening.

In the starlit trees around my Colorado home, I hear many sounds of nature – the yearning song of a frog, the ferocious snarl of a bobcat or the swoosh of wind in the boughs of a spruce. My favourite sound, though, is the call of a great horned owl. Deep, gentle, insistent, it echoes through the woods, asking, 'Who are you, who?'

Nature not only poses that question, it helps me to find the answer. Walking through a grove of towering trees, sitting beside a tumbling mountain stream or breathing the salty scent of the sea . . . nature opens up all my senses. I feel, at once, more alive, more aware and more grateful.

And that's only the beginning. In the hardest times of my life, nature has given me lasting gifts – renewing my spirits, calming my mind and healing my aching heart. As weighty and overwhelming as our troubles might seem, nature can, somehow, hold them all.

For nature is a living circle whose embrace is everywhere, all around us, all the time. That's why people from every place and time have expressed their love of nature. So deep and enduring is that love, it's found in every form of human expression – from ancient cave paintings to modern music. It's revealed in our cherished stories, paintings, poems, films, rituals, sand mandalas, sculptures, symphonies, ballads, dances, gardens and blessings.

Love of nature is also found in one more form – one that's often overlooked: the names we choose for living things.

Those names are right here, whispering seductively in our ears, eager to share their secrets. They are embedded in every language and culture. They are so ubiquitous, they are easily missed, gemstones hiding in plain sight. Or, worse, they are too easily forgotten, as modern humans grow less aware of nature, less connected to its rhythms and less inspired by its wonders. Yet those names tell fabulous tales – if only we can hear them.

Names like ... meadowlark, wunderpus, sarcastic fringehead, halcyon, timberdoodle, ghost crab, hellbender, foxglove, axolotl, elephant, leafy sea dragon, boondaburra, kiss-me-over-the-garden-gate, morpho butterfly, gooseneck barnacle, narwhal, pumpkin toadlet and dragonfly. And let's not forget koala, nudibranch, dugong, humuhumunukunukuapua'a, yeti, sempervirens, vampire squid, paikea, chimpanzee and (one of my all-time favourites) resplendent quetzal.

By knowing these names, we breathe life into them. In doing so, we also breathe life into those astonishing creatures themselves.

Naming inspires attention. Attention inspires passion. And passion inspires connection.

That is why this book explores nature through the names we have given to myriad other forms of life. What have we called them, and why? What meanings do those names hold? And what do they reveal about ourselves, the namers? For each and every name has a unique story – often amazing, frequently surprising, sometimes tragic, always illuminating.

You'll notice that this book is organised in an unusual way. Instead of sticking to the traditional taxonomic labels for creatures and plants, I've taken a more playful, appreciative approach. Why? Because this book isn't a scientific text. Rather, it's a celebration of the wondrous array of life on this planet, seen through the lens of nature's marvellous names.

Throughout my life, I've been blessed with two constant companions – love of language and love of nature. Those two qualities have flowed together in this book, pouring into every page, and they've combined in many surprising ways I couldn't have imagined. I hope they will enrich your journey as much as they have mine.

Now, a note of caution: with so many life forms, languages and traditions to choose from, this book is necessarily incomplete. (On top of that, we're discussing only the fascinating names of living things, not the equally fascinating names of places.) As a result, this book can explore only the tiniest fraction of a subset of a microcosm of all the possibilities of names in nature. While I've done my best to choose some of the most wonderful, radiant and evocative ones . . . it's still just a sampling.

We are, in other words, attempting to view an ocean of wonders through just a few drops of seawater. A nearly impossible task. And yet, if seen in the right light, each drop will evoke the wider glory. The deeper mystery. The greater miracle.

Finally, this celebration of nature holds a heartfelt plea. As we enjoy and appreciate nature – let's also do more to protect it. Every choice we make matters. So let's resolve to make choices that are more wise, more loving and more gracious.

Protecting our fellow creatures isn't a new idea. It's found in ancient tales all around the world. Consider the biblical tale of Noah's Ark. That magnificent story isn't only about the power of faith – it's also about the value of nature. In other words: if God asked Noah to go to so much trouble to save all those creatures . . . how can we possibly do any less?

What's new about this idea today is the urgency. Some of the names you will find in these pages belong to creatures whose very existence is now endangered. In this era of alarming decline of biodiversity, we must do more to protect other kinds of life. Not only for them but for us. Because saving nature is also saving ourselves.

Let's ask ourselves: Do we choose to live as consumers – devouring nature for short-term benefit? Or do we choose to live as good stewards – living in long-term harmony with our fellow creatures and the planet that sustains us all?

My highest hope for this book is that it will feel, to you, like a lovely invitation. To enter into nature and let its magic seep into your soul. To breathe deeply its fragrant mix of beauty, renewal, mystery and awe. For we belong to this living circle whose embrace is everywhere, all around us, all the time.

T. A. B.

CHAPTER 1

High Fliers

Higher still and higher...

The blue deep thou wingest,

And singing still dost soar, and soaring ever singest

PERCY BYSSHE SHELLEY, 'TO A SKYLARK'

PHAROMACHRUS MOCINNO

Resplendent Quetzal

A flash of bright, iridescent colours in the rainforest of Central America could be one of the world's most glorious birds: a resplendent quetzal. Brilliant turquoise, green and scarlet feathers decorate these birds' long, opulent tails. Like jewels glistening among the trees, they shimmer and glow, seeming to radiate their own light. Which is why they truly deserve to be called 'resplendent', a word that comes from the Latin *resplendens*, meaning 'shining' and 'splendid'.

The name 'quetzal' originated with the Aztec language Nahuatl, whose word *quetzalli* means 'precious feathers'. (Nahuatl, by the way, is still spoken today by around 2 million people in Mexico.) And 'precious' is an appropriate description, for the highly prized feathers of these birds have long symbolised wisdom and power. Additionally, quetzals evoke a strong connection to the Mesoamerican god Quetzalcoatl – a powerful creator god resembling a feathered serpent. In traditional Mesoamerican lore, Quetzalcoatl was credited with many marvels, including the invention of the calendar, the development of farming and even the creation of humanity.

The first time I ever saw a resplendent quetzal, on a journey through Costa Rica, I wasn't expecting to see anything so spectacular. I was simply appreciating the many shades of green in the thick canopy of leaves over my head. Focusing my binoculars on a particular branch that arched upwards, like a leafy arm reaching towards the sky, I followed its graceful curve higher. All of a sudden – a vivid flash of turquoise exploded in my vision. A resplendent quetzal!

For a long while, I stood there, watching the bird's feathers glow with ethereal intensity. Completely oblivious to my presence, it continued to move along the branch, pausing every now and

1875 | John Gould | *Pharomachrus mocinno*

then to open a gleaming wing or shake itself with a bright burst of colours. Eventually, it moved high enough that the leaves obscured it completely. For me, watching it vanish, it felt like seeing the blazing sun set at the end of the day.

Sadly, the future for these birds does not look as bright as their feathers. Their numbers are declining due to human activities, especially deforestation, which continue to shrink their habitat. For now, at least, these radiant birds remain part of our world – and a miraculously beautiful part, as well.

STURNELLA NEGLECTA

Meadowlark

To the Indigenous Americans of the Cheyenne tribes, the meadowlark is called *méséhávo'o*, meaning 'bird of the dawn'. What better name could there be for this bird whose bright voice announces the morning?

To the people of the Lakota Sioux, the meadowlark is called *tasiyagnunpa*, a name that signifies this bird's essential role in Lakota tradition: to sing of all the good in the universe. The Lakota speak evocatively in their lore about meadowlarks, even suggesting that meadowlarks speak the language of the Lakota. Perhaps the birds are discussing the people, even as the people are discussing the birds? In this lovely way, a connection across species has taken the form of a living circle of story.

My own mother loved the sweetly spiralling songs from these iconic birds of the American West. She celebrated their songs every spring in Colorado. As she observed, 'To be joyful, just listen to a meadowlark.' Some mornings in April and May, she'd get up before dawn and slip quietly through the meadow grasses as the first rays of sunlight touched the landscape with

c. 1830 | John James Audubon | *Sturnella neglecta*

golden light. Always mindful to avoid stepping on an early blooming, light purple pasque flower, which she liked to call 'the prairie crocus', she would find a spot in the middle of a field. And there she'd stand, as still as a ponderosa pine, waiting hopefully to hear the sound that would ring with joy. The song of a meadowlark.

Alas, western meadowlarks, once so common, are now imperiled; threatened by shrinking habitats as well as deadly pesticides. If they were to vanish, it would be as if someone had ripped a gaping hole in the soundscape of the American West. At this point, their future is uncertain, their prospects as tenuous as the last, lilting note of a cherished song.

ALCEDINIDAE

Halcyon Bird

This poetic English name for a variety of kingfishers is quite different from the purely descriptive names in French and German. The French name *martin-pêcheur* conveys that these birds are good at catching fish, while the German name *eisvogel*, which translates as 'ice bird', refers to their striking blue plumage.

The English name 'halcyon bird', by contrast, isn't meant to be descriptive. It hails from a poignant Greek myth, a beautiful story of grievous tragedy and enduring love. The tale revolves around Alcyone, a princess of Thessaly and the daughter of the god of the winds, Aeolus. (Incidentally, Aeolus' name is the root of the term 'aeolian harp', a beautiful musical instrument whose strings vibrate with the wind.) Although there are several different versions of the story, they all agree on one point: Alcyone and her husband, Ceyx, were deeply in love and lived

1883 | Archibald Thorburn | *Alcedinidae*

1861 | John Gould | *Metallura primolina*

together blissfully – until, unexpectedly, Ceyx perished in a storm at sea. Utterly devastated, Alcyone couldn't be consoled. So intense was her grief that at last, she hurled herself into the ocean to drown.

Moved by this tragedy, the gods transformed them both into sea birds – kingfishers, called *halkyōn* in Greek or *halcyon* in Latin. Additionally, to allow Alcyone to build a nest that could rest safely on top of the waves, her father promised to calm the ocean winds every year at the time of the winter solstice. For several weeks around that time, the ocean winds subside so that Alcyone can make her nest upon the surface. Ever since, those sublime days of peace and tranquility at sea are called 'halcyon days'. Today, the phrase refers to any time of peace, joy and prosperity.

TROCHILIDAE

Hummingbird

Spectacularly colourful, capable of intricate aerial acrobatics and so courageous that ancient Aztec warriors wore their feathers into battle, hummingbirds are winged miracles. Throughout time and across diverse cultures, they have been celebrated and admired. And rightly so. No other kind of bird can beat its wings up to eighty times per second, producing that distinctive hum. Or hover in the air, perfectly positioned to sip nectar from a flower. Or fly backwards and even upside down. Not only that, these tiny feathered jewels (some of which weigh less than 2 grammes, the weight of a penny) are also amazingly sturdy. Some hummingbirds migrate almost 6,300 kilometres (4,000 miles) each year, flying from Alaska to Mexico and back again – crossing mountain ranges, wide prairies and open seas.

What glorious names in English their iridescent wings have inspired! The names for hummingbird species deserve to be spoken aloud, as if they were poetry – and visualised, as if they were paintings: glittering-bellied emerald. Amethyst woodstar. Red-tailed comet. Green-crowned woodnymph. Horned sungem. Fiery-throated metaltail. Rainbow-bearded thornbill. That's only a small sampling of the evocative names for these birds. But my favourite hummingbird name is the Spanish word for the smallest kind of all, a tiny creature known in English as the 'bee hummingbird'. In Spanish, this little wonder is called *zunzuncito*. That should be said with enthusiasm, as if it were an exclamation. *Zunzuncito!* Say it out loud – and you'll hear a name that truly buzzes with the sound of whirring wings.

In many European languages, the word for hummingbird is rooted in Taíno, an indigenous language of the Caribbean. The Taíno term for hummingbird, *colibri*, is found in Czech *kolibrić*, German *kolibri*, Polish *koliber* and Basque *kolibria*. So this name, like many hummingbirds, has migrated across enormous distances.

DIOMEDEIDAE
Albatross

These champions of the sky ride the winds across wide expanses of ocean, soaring up to 16,000 kilometres (10,000 miles) in a single flight. That's the equivalent of travelling 40 per cent of the circumference of the earth, or about three times the distance from New York City to London. Or more than twice the distance between Tokyo and Sydney.

Unknown | *Diomedea exulans*

How is such a feat possible? The answer is the albatross's enormous wingspan. Measured from tip to tip, their wings stretch up to 3.7 metres (12 feet) in length. Such enormous wings enable these birds to glide for months – sometimes even years – without landing on solid ground. Entire seasons may pass without an albatross planting its feet on anything resembling soil or sand. Occasionally, they will come to rest on open water, feed on small fish and then return to their lives in the air, soaring on high.

Like the bird itself, its varied names have flown far and wide. 'Albatross' originated with the Arabic words *al-qādūs* and *al-ġaṭṭās*, which may have also applied to other large waterbirds, including pelicans and frigate birds. Many people in the South Pacific call albatrosses 'mollymawks', which probably comes from 'mallemugge', the Dutch name for another kind of seabird. Meanwhile, sailors in other places sometimes call them 'gooney birds', a rather unlikely name for these graceful riders of the ocean winds.

The scientific name for the genus of albatrosses, *Diomedea*, is taken from Diomedes, the Greek hero of the Trojan War, who took the city's sacred Palladium and also rode inside the Trojan Horse. While Diomedes survived that great battle, many of his loyal companions did not. According to legend, they became birds that were destined to soar endlessly above the sea cliffs, never touching the land.

Many myths have ridden on the wings of albatrosses over the centuries. British, Dutch, French and Portuguese sailors once believed that these majestic birds were the spirits of drowned sailors, returned to life in new form, soaring safely above the ocean waves rather than perilously sailing them. Others claimed that albatrosses brought good luck to voyagers at sea, and even held magical healing powers. To those believers, the merest glance of an albatross could bring good fortune to an entire shipload of sailors. Still others considered albatrosses the living symbols of enduring love.

No wonder that British sailors who harmed albatrosses were traditionally condemned as bringing bad luck, even doom, to themselves and their shipmates. That's why the sailor so vividly portrayed by Samuel Taylor Coleridge in his epic poem, *The Rime of the Ancient Mariner*, had to wear around his neck the carcass of an albatross he'd killed. Such was his punishment, equal parts torment and humiliation. To this day, when someone behaves so badly they deserve terrible scorn, it's often said they are wearing an albatross around their neck.

ARCHBOLDIA PAPUENSIS

Bowerbird

Deep in the remote rainforests of Papua New Guinea, and also in the eucalyptus groves of Australia, lives one of nature's most accomplished architects, the bowerbird. To watch one of them at work is to witness genuine artistry – as well as surprising skill.

A male will labour mightily to build a durable structure out of woven sticks, carefully painted with saliva, hoping to catch the eye of a female. While that construction project is, by itself, an impressive feat, he has only begun to display his creative talents. For he then takes great pains to adorn the structure with elaborate arrays of colourful objects such as stones, flowers and shells. (No doubt, if he had access to glittering jewellery or luminous chandeliers, he'd make use of them, too.) Each decorative object is selected and positioned with supreme care. The female will often watch all this activity with seeming indifference. She takes it all in, observing the homes made by her suitors as well as their theatrical mating dances, until finally she will choose her mate.

The word 'bower' comes from the Old High German *būan,* meaning 'to dwell'. At some point along the way, that word melded with the Old English term *bēon,* meaning 'to be'. Ultimately, all this evolved into the word we recognise today, 'bower'.

Appropriately, this same word was used for centuries to describe the private chamber of a European medieval lady. Whenever a lady retired to her bower, she was not to be disturbed without special permission, for that place was meant to be a personal refuge. The term 'bower' was also sometimes used to refer to an attractive shelter in a medieval garden, normally made from woven branches and vines. Much like the lady's chamber, this shelter was a special, protected, private place. Under either definition, the word 'bower' is a fitting choice for the name of this

c. 1895 | Richard Bowdler Sharpe | *Archboldia papuensis*

1837 | John Gould | *Regulus regulus*

bird, which is so highly accomplished in designing and building an appealing home for his mate.

In the Australian habitat of these birds, the Indigenous Wiradjuri people have called them by a different name, *ngurumbula*, for thousands of years. This means 'two homes', because, as well as the elaborate courtship bower, bowerbirds typically construct a sturdy nest nearby, where females can safely lay their eggs. As versatile avian architects, they build varied structures. Who knows what they might build next?

REGULUS REGULUS

Goldcrest

The diminutive goldcrest is the smallest bird in Europe, only just over 8 or 9 centimetres (3 inches) long. But don't let its size, smaller than the palm of your hand, fool you. For this bird carries a name weighty with tradition and ringing with royalty: *Regulus,* the scientific name for this petite bird, means 'little king'. And that term has been adopted not just by the scientific community but also by people throughout Europe. In fact, the goldcrest is called a royal bird in many languages. For example, its Norwegian name is *fuglekongen*, or 'bird king'.

Why should this tiny bird merit such royal treatment? To be sure, it wears a crest of golden feathers on its head, somewhat like a crown. But is there something more than that going on here?

As is often the case with the names of our fellow creatures, the answer lies in traditional sources. In this case, the origin of the goldcrest's regal status is an ancient Greek folktale dating back all the way to Aristotle.

In the tale, birds from everywhere gathered on a momentous occasion – to settle the question, for all time, of which could fly the highest. So they organised a contest where every bird would have the opportunity to fly as high into the sky as it possibly could. The winner would be declared, with glorious celebration, the king of all birds.

As the birds gathered for the contest, the air vibrated with their wings. The excitement was palpable. Feathers of every colour imaginable shimmered in the bright sunlight. Some birds, especially the raptors that could soar far above the landscape, felt very confident. Others, like the songbirds that lived in marshes and forests, fretted nervously.

Amid the throng, there was one bird so small that few others even noticed it was there. That bird strolled quietly among the others, looking for something in particular. It wasn't considering its odds of success. That clever little bird was simply considering its plan. Stealthily, it moved closer to the biggest, strongest raptor – a great eagle. Impressive by any measure, the eagle was snapping its beak in anticipation of victory, shaking its golden feathers and stretching its enormous muscular wings to their full length.

In that moment, the little bird did something very brave. It leapt onto the eagle's wing and burrowed itself in the feathers.

A cry rose up and the contest began. All the birds lifted off, beating their wings vigorously, climbing higher and higher into the sky. The great eagle pumped its wings powerfully, rising above the others, just as it had expected. Soon enough, it had surpassed everyone else. Clucking with satisfaction, it knew that it had, indeed, flown higher than any other bird. When, at last, it could no longer make itself beat its tired wings, the eagle released a proud cry of victory that echoed across the lands below. It began to drift back down, certain that it had triumphed.

At that instant, its tiny passenger suddenly emerged. With a burst of strength, the little bird flapped its wings energetically. Climbing still higher, it called out in its own high-pitched voice, loud enough that all the other birds could hear. For the little one knew that it had, in fact, flown higher than anyone else.

And that's how a very small flier won the contest and became the king of all the birds. Which is why, to this day, that regal bird wears a golden crown.

PTEROPTOCHOS TARNII

Huet-Huet

Some birds are heard far more often than they are seen. That could be the case because they are nocturnal, or because they live in remote places, or because they are simply very cautious and keep themselves well hidden. Whatever the reason, it's the unique calls and songs of these birds, rather than their brightly painted wings or extraordinary habits, that announce them to the world. And some of them have become so completely identified with their calls that they have names mimicking those sounds.

Those onomatopoeic names have always intrigued me, tickling my ears as well as my fancy. Something about a bird speaking its own name, while remaining invisible, feels so audacious. As if it's daring anyone in earshot to find its secret hiding place. One of my favourite birds with an onomatopoeic name is the huet-huet, which lives deep in the Patagonian forests of Chile and Argentina. While I've been lucky enough to hear one many times, making the distinctive *huet-huet* call that's also its Spanish name, I've never actually seen one. Not once. As a result, this bird feels a bit like a phantom of the forest. All I have known is its lovely call, gentle, alluring and mysterious.

1833 | Alcide Dessalines d'Orbigny | *Pteroptochos tarnii*

Patagonia is home to several other birds named evocatively for their calls, including a passerine named *chucao*, an owl called *tucúquere* and a woodpecker known as *pitio*. Whenever you hear those calls, you can tell exactly which birds are nearby, even if they're completely unseen.

But perhaps the best-known bird whose name imitates its call is the cuckoo. Found in Europe, Asia and Africa, it has inspired plenty of stories and songs across diverse cultures, always accompanied by *cuckoo, cuckoo*. That includes the Greek myth in which Zeus becomes a cuckoo to seduce Hera; the Celtic legend in which cuckoos have the power to call beyond our world to the spirits of the dead; and the plays of Shakespeare in which cuckoos symbolise adultery – a connection that springs from the birds' habit of laying their eggs in other birds' nests. (Which is, by the way, the root of the word 'cuckold'.)

Finally, I can't resist mentioning one more example of a bird with a name taken from its call: the boobook. This tiny little owl lives in the forests of Australia, New Zealand and New Guinea (with close relatives in India, Malaysia, Singapore, Thailand and Vietnam). The owl's gentle nighttime calls of *boobook, boobook* echo hauntingly through the trees. Even its scientific name, *Ninox boobook*, was inspired by that voice. Originally named by Aboriginal Australians of the Yuin-Kuric group, the name, like the call, has clearly been appreciated by people for thousands of years.

It's very good, in our noisy and tumultuous times, to remember the enduring power of that call. Even a quiet voice spoken by a tiny creature in a remote place can reach across vast distances of space and time.

LIPAUGUS VOCIFERANS
Screaming Piha

This bird absolutely deserves its name. While some creatures bear appellations that have been inspired by their distinctive colour or shape or habitat, this one is named for the sound of its voice. For the screaming piha is by far the loudest bird in the Amazon rainforest. Shrieking a three-note song that's impossible to miss, this bird has become the most recognisable voice of the region. Because of the shrillness of its cries, the screaming piha's call easily slices through the thick forest growth, rising above the rest of the cacophony. Thanks to that voice, an unremarkable-looking grey bird is still able to make an unforgettable impression.

As you might expect, the bird's scientific name refers to the significance (and the volume) of its voice. So scientists have labelled this rainforest resident *Vociferans*, the Latin term for 'noisy'. In the languages of the region, the bird's name is also based on its piercing cries. In Colombia, for example, the bird's Spanish name is *guardabosque chillón*, which means 'screeching loud ranger'. Meanwhile, in Brazil, the bird's Portuguese name simply imitates its call, *cricrió*.

Why, you might ask, has this bird evolved to make such a jarringly loud cry? As is often the case in nature, it's in the valuable service of attracting a mate. That screaming voice not only helps potential couples to locate each other in the dense growth of the forest, but it also could actually be perceived as attractive. Maybe, to another piha that is looking for a mate, the more loud, shrill and harsh, the better? (Alas, for any potential mate that happens to prefer peace and quiet around the nest... tough luck.)

1836 | William Swainson | *Lipaugus vociferans*

1851 | Charles Frederic DuBois | *Falco columbarius*

FALCO COLUMBARIUS
Merlin

This falcon may be small in size, but it's very large in attitude. Which also makes it a formidable foe, a ferocious hunter and an inspiring creature to watch. A merlin flies with confidence and power.

In a wonderful example of the surprising evolution of names, that name also carries a very different sort of power. For the same name figures prominently in the realm of legend. Merlin as a figure of lore is the original wizard, and he remains one of the world's most beloved characters. For well over a thousand years, he has inspired magical tales, songs, plays, films, paintings and poems in almost every language. But is there any connection between the name of the wizard and the name of the bird?

First, let's look at the linguistic path of the bird's name. It evolved originally from *smiril*, an early German word for 'falcon' or 'hawk' that dates back many centuries. That word led eventually to the Old French term *esmerillon*, which ultimately morphed into the modern *merlin*.

Meanwhile, the Merlin of Celtic lore first appeared in ancient Welsh oral traditions more than 1,300 years ago. Those tales featured Myrddin Wyllt, or 'Myrddin of the Wild', a wise old bard who lived in the forests of Wales. According to legend, this man of nature often spoke with the animals and trees. (And, on occasion, with humans.) His name, Myrddin, arose from the Celtic words for 'sea' and 'hill', which combined to make the term *Mori-dunon*. Over time, *Mori-dunon* evolved into Myrddin and, later, into Merlin. By the time the cleric Geoffrey of Monmouth wrote about him in his *Prophetiæ Merlini* and *Historia Regum Britanniae*, the wizard Merlin had already been celebrated in legend for centuries.

Thus, even though both uses of the name have been around for a very long time, it's likely they had different origins. Yet it's fair to say that they share more than a name. The merlin falcon is beautiful in flight, and people have long admired its power and grace. Likewise, after many centuries, the stories of Merlin the wizard continue to soar.

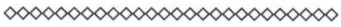

HERPSILOCHMUS PRAEDICTUS

Predicted Antwren

In addition to being close observers of nature and intrepid explorers, wildlife biologists are also skilled sleuths. Think of Sherlock Holmes tracking an elusive suspect deep in a remote tropical rainforest – but instead of wearing his trademark deerstalker cap and inverness coat (wool being a bit too warm for the tropics), modern wildlife biologists wear sun hats and lightweight clothing that can quickly dry after torrential rains or river crossings. In place of the famous calabash pipe and magnifying glass, they carry excellent binoculars, cameras and sophisticated mapping technology. And rather than hailing from a comfortable detective's office in London, they return to a research lab affiliated with a university, government agency or non-profit organisation.

Yet beyond those differences, their quests would be truly parallel. They would both search their surroundings carefully and ingeniously, aiming to seek out hidden clues, gain understanding through reasoning and make new discoveries. On rare occasions, they might even find a secretive suspect – one whose identity had never before been revealed.

Wildlife biologists exploring the Amazon rainforest of Brazil in 2013 did exactly that. After discovering clues that indicated a new species of bird in the region, they speculated that it was probably a kind of antwren. They also concluded, based on their observations, that it would likely be found somewhere near the Madeira River. They named this yet-to-be-documented bird the 'predicted antwren'.

Now, antwrens are not the easiest birds to find – even if you know exactly what you're looking for. They're petite, smaller than your fist and they live in thick forests, often concealed by shadows. Sometimes they're revealed only by a few notes of song. To find them, you could say, takes excellent sleuth work.

Which is what those wildlife biologists did. The new species of bird was ultimately found in the expected location. Taxonomists gave it the scientific name *Herpsilochmus praedictus*, with the first word describing a bird that inhabits dense forest growth, and the second word meaning – appropriately – 'predicted'.

Wherever he hangs his deerstalker cap these days, Sherlock Holmes must be pleased.

CINCLUS MEXICANUS

Water Ouzel

Few birds have such a delightful name as the water ouzel, the only aquatic songbird native to North America. Just saying the name out loud is enough to make me smile.

On top of that, few birds have such a delightful way of feeding themselves. It's guaranteed entertainment to watch one plunge into a mountain stream or a waterfall in search of insects, larvae or worms. Sometimes it might dine while swimming on the surface, and sometimes it will dive underwater, using its wings to manoeuvre through the currents. No wonder it was the favourite bird of John Muir, explorer of California's Sierra Nevada mountains in the 1800s. He described it as 'a singularly joyous and lovable little fellow . . . flitting about in the spray, diving in foaming eddies, whirling like a leaf'.

The bird's colloquial name came from its resemblance to the Eurasian blackbird, also called ouzel or ousel. That bird's name originated from the Old English word *osle*, which meant 'blackbird', which itself came from the ancient German word *amsel*. Most likely, that word grew from the even older Indo-European term *ams*, meaning 'black'.

Yet despite its resemblance to the Eurasian blackbird, the water ouzel is not truly related. In fact, they belong to entirely different families. So to eliminate any confusion, ornithologists changed the water ouzel's name to the American dipper. That new name refers to the bird's unusual habit of bobbing vigorously before it plunges into water. While the new name is more accurate scientifically, it is, alas, much less charming.

That charm remains, though, in the Indigenous American names for this bird. To the Yup'ik tribe of Alaska, it's known as *puyuqumaar(aq*)*, meaning 'the little bird that looks like smoke'. Meanwhile, to the Inupiat, it's called *arnaq kiviruq*. That can be translated as 'woman sinking', referring to how the bird drops into the waterways of the Far North.

And that's not all. The collective term for a group of water ouzels is 'a ladle of dippers'. To my mind, that conjures an image of a huge ladle that could scoop up several of these water-loving creatures at once from a tumbling stream.

TACHYCINETA LEUCOPYGA
Pilmaiquen

'Spirits that fly'. That's the rather lyrical meaning of *pilmaiquen*, the name given by South America's Mapuche tribe to the birds most commonly known today as 'swallows'. The Mapuche admired swallows enough to believe that these aerial acrobats were truly spirits with wings. That South American tribe is certainly not alone in celebrating swallows. People around the globe have long cherished these birds that dart and soar so swiftly. Today, these birds can be found all across Europe, Africa, Asia and the Americas. In some parts of the world, such as Japan, people even mark their seasons by the swallows' migrations.

In sum, there's vast appreciation worldwide for these birds. And the various collective terms in English for a flock of swallows reveal that appreciation. As a group, swallows are called 'a richness', 'a swoop', 'a flight' or (if the flock is hungrily dining on insects) 'a gulp'.

In China, it's believed that a swallow nesting at your home can protect you and your family from serious evil. Meanwhile, British sailors traditionally viewed the bird as a symbol of hope for their safety. In Estonia, where swallows are the national bird, some folk say that anyone who kills a swallow will lose their sight forever.

A swallow appears in a proverb attributed to Aristotle, and another is featured in one of *Aesop's Fables*. In the Greek myth of Procne, she endured terrible suffering until, at last, the gods finally transformed her into a swallow.

Some of the most compelling legends about them come from Indigenous American cultures. One Hopi story tells of a swallow that prevented humans from starving by bringing them a precious seed of corn, saving all of humanity. In another Indigenous American tale, a barn swallow steals fire from the gods to help humanity. But its tail was burned in the escape, leaving it permanently damaged – which is why barn swallows to this day have forked tails.

In the traditions of Abrahamic religions, these birds are revered symbols of faith as well as divine protection. In Jewish tradition, for example, swallows represent spiritual freedom as well as God's devotion. In Kabbalistic literature, swallows are likened to the souls of righteous believers. Islamic teachings see the migrations of these birds as a reminder to surrender completely to God's wisdom. And in Christian tradition, swallows may symbolise Christ's Incarnation; a swallow came to comfort Jesus upon the cross. Moreover, the Bible speaks of swallows to remind us of God's divine care, the eternal grace that protects all living creatures.

c. 1890 | Richard Bowdler Sharpe | *Tachycineta leucopyga*

1881 | Edwin Sheppard | *Scolopax minor*

SCOLOPAX MINOR

Timberdoodle

This shorebird, found across eastern North America, surely has one of the goofiest names in all of nature. But while the first known use was in an 1839 magazine article about bird hunting, which cited timberdoodles as game birds, the origins of the term are a mystery.

Officially called in English 'the American woodcock', these birds have been given other names by Indigenous peoples. To the Cree tribe, they are *papakapittesis* ('little speckled creatures'). To the Abenaki people, meanwhile, they have long been known as *nagwibagw sibs* ('under leaf birds').

Woodcocks also have many other entertaining nicknames. In various North American locales, they may be called 'hokumpoke', 'mudbat', 'Labrador twister', 'night partridge', or – the least complimentary option – 'bog sucker'. But my personal favourite remains, by far, 'timberdoodle'.

What explains all these varied names? Maybe they were inspired by this bird's fascinating display dances, which are just as whimsical and comical as its names. Those dances are unforgettable sights to witness. To attract the attention of females, male birds shuffle along the turf, all the while rocking their whole bodies rhythmically. Then they fly upwards in a graceful, looping spiral, twittering and chirping harmoniously before finally dropping back down to the ground. This performance, both bizarre and beautiful, is truly one of nature's most memorable rituals. So why not pair it with an equally memorable name?

An Encounter with Sandhill Cranes

Birds have flown through my life on many occasions, their feathery wings often brushing my heart. Wherever I've wandered, magnificent birds have renewed my spirits and rekindled my wonder. It happened in Kenya, when I watched thousands of flamingos settle like a long pink ribbon on the shores of Lake Nakuru. It happened in Antarctica, when a pair of albatrosses danced together with elegance and intricacy. In the Himalayas, when a small group of black-necked cranes rested after their long journey across the mountains from Tibet. In Australia, when the wings of rainbow lorikeets gathered in a nearby tree, their wings aglow like radiant prisms.

Yet no experience with birds could ever surpass one that happened quite close to my home in the American West – my first sighting of sandhill cranes. Each year, around 1 million of these grand creatures migrate from the northernmost parts of Alaska to Mexico, and back again. And most of them settle down briefly in March on a short stretch of Nebraska's Platte River, a waterway that local old-timers describe as 'a mile wide and an inch deep'.

Cranes are striking birds, standing very tall (about 1.3 metres/4 feet 6 inches), with sabre-sharp bills and splashes of red on their heads.

Their lean, angular shape makes them look almost like pterodactyls that flew straight out of an ancient fossil bed and landed in modern Nebraska. In fact, there is fossil evidence that these birds have existed in North America for millions of years.

Most impressive to me is their call. Sandhill cranes make a throaty, trumpeting cry that can echo far across the prairies and mountains, ringing in the rising sun. Something about that passionate cry seems older than old, vibrating with Earth's earliest music, as if the cranes are calling not only across vast stretches of distance – but also across vast stretches of time.

One morning before dawn, my wife and I crept quietly down to an old duck blind near the Platte River. The air smelled of marshes and waterbirds. As the first rays of dawn light touched the reeds and cattails growing along the riverbank, the cranes began to stir. As if a vast down comforter were being shaken, rippling across the river, thousands upon thousands of cranes were shaking their immense wings, splashing the water, stepping through the shallows, dancing energetically and releasing their ancient calls. Joined by even greater numbers of other migratory birds – ducks and cormorants and swans and geese, plus one lone whooping crane that had joined the throng – the sandhill cranes greeted the new day.

CHAPTER 2

Wonders of the Water

It's as strange
as a leafy sea dragon
– nature's camouflage
worn with elegance.

MAGGIE STIEFVATER, *THE SCORPIO RACES*

MITSUKURINA OWSTONI
Goblin Shark

Deep in the waters of Japan swim these rather spooky creatures with savage teeth, enormous jaws and protruding noses: goblin sharks.

These predators cruise the depths searching for prey, just as they and their ancestors have done for the last 125 million years. Using their noses, which are extremely sensitive electroreceptors, to discern the slightest changes in electrical fields from other organisms nearby, they slowly glide closer to their target – until they are finally within striking distance. Then all at once, they attack. They bite with incredible speed, burying their fang-like teeth deep into their prey. Game over.

The name 'goblin shark' is a rough translation of the Japanese word *tenguzame*, which was inspired by the tengu, a mythical being long celebrated in Japanese folklore. Whether found in the ancient Shinto temples of Shikoku or in the modern films of Hayao Miyazaki, this legendary being is half man, half bird and completely ferocious. Tengus are often portrayed with a scarlet face and an especially sharp nose. Devious, mischievous and capable of good or evil, they are as unpredictable as they are dangerous. Like any respectable goblin, they should definitely be avoided.

1949 | John Roxborough Norman | *Mitsukurina owstoni*

Fortunately, for humans at least, that's not difficult to do. These sharks live at such great depths that encounters with people are extremely rare. In fact, the most common way they've been seen is when they get entangled in fishing nets that catch them (along with many other unfortunate creatures) in deep waters. Against those nets, even a goblin is powerless.

PHYCODURUS EQUES

Leafy Sea Dragon

Surely one of nature's most elegant and lavishly dressed creatures, the leafy sea dragon lives in the tropical waters of Australia's Great Barrier Reef. Look at them closely and you'll see long, floaty shapes covering the bony surface of their bodies, making them resemble tiny dragons decked out for a costume ball.

But you might never look at them so closely. In fact, you might not notice them at all. That's because their lavish dress is strictly for camouflage. They resemble – with impressive accuracy – mere loose pieces of seaweed. They seem so unremarkable, so uninteresting, that most potential predators simply swim right past them. To complete their seaweed disguise, leafy sea dragons also have transparent fins that whir invisibly, helping them to glide through the water much like leaves adrift. No wonder the local folk simply call these creatures 'leafies'.

1885 | Frederick McCoy | *Phycodurus eques*

While their English name of 'leafy sea dragon' does fit them perfectly, it doesn't convey how much these fish also resemble horses. For they truly could be small, flamboyantly attired steeds that gracefully ride the currents of the sea. That's why I also cherish the name used by the Noongar Boodjar, an Aboriginal Australian people. For thousands of years, they have called these tiny creatures *mamoongat ngoort*, meaning 'ocean horses'.

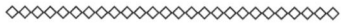

CHROMODORIDIDAE

Nudibranch

Are they really nude? That, of course, is the essential question about these bizarre and truly dazzling creatures.

The answer is ... sort of. These marine molluscs have developed gills outside of their main bodies, often resembling plumes or horns on their backs. As they breathe through those gills, the plumes flutter gracefully, waving like tiny flags. So the term 'nudibranch' means 'naked gills'. Like so many names in nature, it's a combination of Latin and Greek – *nudus*, Latin for 'naked', and *bránkhia*, Greek for 'gills'.

Because of their enormous variety and vivid colours, nudibranchs have gained many different nicknames. Those names may have been inspired by their particular hues, their unique shapes, their distinctive ways of moving or their resemblance to other creatures. Some are called 'dancers', others 'dragons' and others 'sea clowns'. Still others are named for their resemblance to adorable rabbits ... or not-so-adorable slugs.

One of my favourite kinds of nudibranch is a blue one – so bright it's almost incandescent – that's found in the waters of the Philippines and Indonesia. This little creature really seems to be lit from within. It has a mouthful of a scientific name, *Chromodoris lochi*. While that name isn't exactly easy to say out loud, I much prefer it to the common name, which is, alas, 'Loch's chromodoris slug'.

Another of my favourites is commonly called 'Spanish dancer' because of its undulating scarlet gills. This glorious nudibranch moves gracefully through the water, sweeping its long, flowing dress behind. And it has a scientific name that's appropriately long and flowing: *Hexabranchus sanguineus*.

The naked facts about nudibranchs are equally impressive. They have proven themselves to be amazingly adaptable. Found on rocks and corals in oceans at every latitude around the globe, they have succeeded at living in widely varied environments. They thrive everywhere from tidal pools at sea level to ocean trenches that are 2,400 metres (8,000 feet) deep. And with several thousand different species spread across the world's oceans, their variations in colour and design are practically infinite.

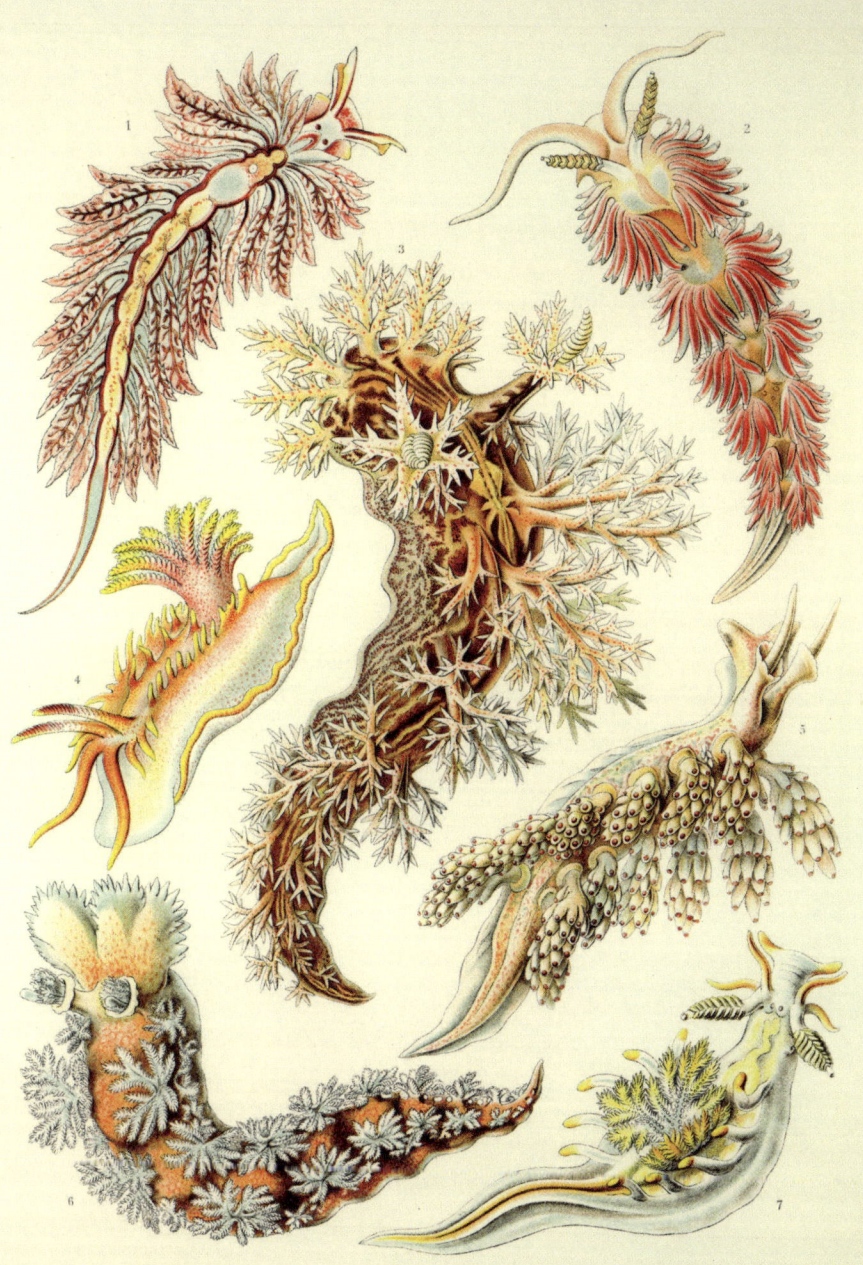

1899 | Ernst Haeckel | *Chromodorididae*

INIA GEOFFRENSIS

Amazon Pink Dolphin

Sleek and graceful, these dolphins swim the great rivers of South America. They're found across the Amazon basin (mainly in Brazil, Bolivia, Peru, Venezuela and Guyana), the Madeira River of Bolivia and the Orinoco basin of Venezuela and Colombia. They eat a wide range of fish and aquatic life – including piranhas (which I sure hope they swallow carefully).

Like all dolphins, they are highly intelligent. They might even be the smartest of all dolphins, having shown remarkable skill at solving problems, along with an unusual degree of awareness of themselves and their environment. It's been suggested by some scientists that they might actually have a kind of moral code that shapes the ways they behave towards each other. In any event, it's interesting – as well as humbling – to note that these dolphins have brains measuring more than a third larger than those of humans.

Amazon pink dolphins are, of course, named for their most striking quality: their lustrous colour. That colour inspired their name not only in English but also in Portuguese (*cor de rosa*) and Spanish (*bufeo colorado*).

1855 | Francis Castelnau | *Inia geoffrensis*

While they start life dull grey, they gradually grow pink, and that hue deepens with time. So these creatures truly grow more beautiful and more vibrant with age. No other dolphins make such a dramatic change in their appearance over the course of their lives. What makes that change possible? It's believed that their marvellous colour is a result of diet and lifestyle, as well as the abundance of capillaries that are near the surface of their skin.

According to Amazonian legend, one of these river dolphins possesses some powerful and dangerous magic. That dolphin, it is said, can shape-shift to make himself look like a man and then stealthily come ashore, hoping to seduce women. He often dons a jaunty hat to conceal the dolphin breathing hole that remains underneath. In the Brazilian version of the tale, the shape-shifter is called *Boto Cor-de-Rosa*, 'the Pink Dolphin', and he always emerges from the river in time to join the festive parties of June. After the parties have ended, he will return to the river and swiftly vanish. In Brazil, to this day, a child whose father is unknown may be called 'the Boto's child'.

While such folktales may add to the notoriety of these creatures, Amazon pink dolphins need nothing more than their own natural qualities to be deemed extraordinary. With their exceptional intelligence and unusual beauty, they are among our most memorable fellow creatures. Alas, they are currently endangered throughout the Amazon region. Their numbers are declining due to mercury pollution from gold mines near their habitats, as well as increased pressures from hunting and development. Time will tell whether the world's only pink dolphins will continue to thrive . . . or vanish forever, rather like the *Boto Cor-de-Rosa*.

AURELIA AURITA
Moon Jelly

Jellyfish fascinated Pliny the Elder, the Roman naturalist who wrote about nature with great erudition and enthusiasm. To him, jellyfish ranked among the world's strangest – and most splendid – creatures. He was particularly intrigued by how they moved through their watery environment by expansion and contraction, a pattern that reminded him very much of breathing. In fact, that unique quality inspired the name he gave to them: *Pulmo marina*, which means 'lungs of the sea'.

Four hundred years earlier, Aristotle had felt the same fascination. But what caught his attention wasn't how jellyfish moved through water, or the typical bell shape of their bodies, but how they could use their tentacles to sting. In light of that ability, he labelled them *cnidae*, the Greek term for 'stinging'. That's why, all these centuries later, the scientific phylum that includes jellyfish is known as *Cnidaria*.

Jellyfish have been thriving on this planet for hundreds of millions of years. Some grow very large – the lion's mane jellyfish has tentacles that can reach over 35 metres (100 feet) in length. They come in a wide array of colours, including blue, pink and yellow, while some of them can produce their own light through the chemical process of bioluminescence.

The collective names for jellyfish are similarly unusual and intriguing. Most commonly, a group of them is called a 'smack', possibly a reference to the painful stings those jellyfish could impart to anyone venturing too close. Some people, however, choose instead to call them a 'smuck'. Who knows why? I've never heard a good explanation, though it's conceivable the term might refer to the sound of stepping on the body of a beached jellyfish. In addition, there are others who prefer to call a group of jellies a 'swarm' or a 'bloom'.

1904 | Ernst Haeckel | *Aurelia aurita*

For most of us, though, jellyfish are notable simply because their appearance resembles... well, jelly. In fact, most of them are composed of 95 per cent water, with the rest being a jelly-like material called mesoglea.

My favourite variety, moon jellies, are round, translucent and alluringly mysterious. They really do resemble delicate, silvery moons. Curiously, in some cultures, they are thought to resemble not moons but ears – hence their names in German (*ohrenqualle*), Russian (*aureliya ushastaya*) and Dutch (*oorkwal*). In any case, these creatures float through the world's oceans, as insubstantial as moonlight on water, glowing with their lovely lunar sheen.

Myths in many languages have been inspired by jellyfish. One of the best is a compelling tale from ancient Japan about a handsome, powerful creature who called himself Kurage. Elegant and majestic, he chose that name because it evoked the words for 'ocean' and 'moon'. But pride ultimately poisoned his mind. In a fit of arrogance, Kurage decided to travel all around the world by himself. Terrible calamities struck on the voyage, battering his body and shattering his mind. He suffered so greatly that he ultimately shrank down until his bones completely disappeared. Returning home, a mere wisp of his former self, he became what we now call a jellyfish, destined to drift aimlessly through the sea for all eternity.

OGCOCEPHALUS DARWINI

Red-Lipped Batfish

Only in the Galápagos.

Those words apply to many amazing creatures, because these volcanic islands off the coast of Ecuador host many forms of life found nowhere else on Earth. The Galápagos are like an enormous treasure chest filled with exotic, wondrous and fascinating jewels. But in this case, the jewels are living, breathing creatures. They include giant tortoises, marine iguanas, tiny penguins, lava lizards, magnificent frigate birds, Darwin's finches, hammerhead sharks, waved albatrosses and Galápagos sea lions.

Of all the bizarre creatures that live on this archipelago, maybe the weirdest of all is the red-lipped batfish. It's like a character from an epic fantasy tale that has somehow come to life in our own world. As you'd expect from the name, these fish have large, fulsome lips that are strikingly bright red. Perhaps, to potential mates, they are also alluring. But other types of fish avoid getting too close. For those lips (as well as the rest of the fish's flesh) are suffused with a poisonous substance that would make for a most unpleasant kiss.

What about the name 'batfish'? That term comes from the fish's flattened, pressed shape – one that is emphasised by its long pectoral fins (which are sturdy enough that the fish can actually use them to walk on the seabed if it chooses). Those fins really do look, when extended, like the wings of bats. Spanish seafarers agree, and also call these fish *pez murciélago labio rojo*, meaning 'batfish with red lips'.

Worth noting, too, is the name used by marine biologists. They call these fish *Ogcocephalus darwini*. While *Ogcocephalus* refers to the creatures' hooked snouts, *darwini* is a salute to Charles Darwin, the brilliant scientist and explorer whose theory of evolution was greatly influenced by his time spent in the Galápagos. For it was there, on those remote islands, that he found creatures as unique as the red-lipped batfish – creatures that have evolved to live in just one place. Only in the Galápagos.

MEGAPTERA NOVAEANGLIAE
Humpback Whale

Nature resounds with lyrical, evocative songs. Many diverse creatures from all around the planet make wonderful music – be they songbirds or wolves, crickets or frogs, elephants or owls. But no creatures' songs are more haunting, or travel so far, as those of humpback whales.

Researchers believe that humpback whale songs, emitted at very low frequencies, can reach more than 16,000 kilometres (10,000 miles). So a humpback whale singing off the sunny coast of Bermuda might be heard in the glacial fjords of Norway, or one singing near Australia's Great Barrier Reef may be audible in the lagoons of French Polynesia. Moreover, these musicians of the deep sea make an enormous variety of sounds, ranging from the delicate whispers between mothers and babies to the majestic songs of adults (which have been recorded singing continuously for twenty-two hours).

They sing, certainly, to communicate important information about their locations, needs or relationships. Perhaps they're also sending messages about their lives and yearnings, hopes and fears. Yet having heard them myself several times, I've been struck by an awareness that there's more going on here than just the exchange of information.

Beneath the elemental beauty of their voices vibrating in the ocean waves, I believe there's also a feeling of joy, a sense of wonder and yes, a touch of gratitude for the miracle of life.

The English common name of these whales refers to the distinctive humped shape of their backs. It's especially visible just before a whale dives down into the depths. For that reason, Hawaiʻians call these whales *kuapiʻo*, which means 'arched back'. *Megaptera*, the scientific name for these whales, focuses on their fins rather than their backs. The term literally means

c. 1920 | Archibald Thorburn | *Megaptera novaeangliae*

'large winged', given because of the huge pectoral fins that extend from their sides like wings.

Sadly, humans have not always lived harmoniously with these magnificent creatures. People once hunted them so aggressively that, less than a century ago, humpback whales nearly vanished from the world forever. Thanks to treaties and international efforts to stop whaling, their numbers are now recovering. But they remain endangered. Today, they face perils from illegal hunting, pollution and entanglement in fishing gear.

To people who have long lived by the oceans with humpback whales, there is deep respect for these intelligent, sensitive and soulful beings. In traditional Hawai'ian culture, for example, they are the sacred embodiment of Kanaloa, god of the sea. Whales also feature in the beloved Hawai'ian song of creation, the Kumulipo. And the annual migration of humpbacks to the islands, a spectacular journey across almost 5,000 kilometres (over 3,000 miles) of ocean, is honoured by Hawai'ians of all ages.

The Māori people of New Zealand also revere humpback whales. Embedded in their culture are rich traditions of whale riding. The Māoris call these whales *paikea*, after a mythical explorer named Kahutia-te-rangi who arrived in New Zealand on the back of a whale and later transformed himself into a whale to explore the oceans. In early Māori carvings, the legendary explorer looks very much indeed like a humpback whale.

Perhaps, if we listen well enough, we might be able to hear, in those ancient carvings and creation stories, the haunting echoes of whale songs.

WONDERS OF THE WATER

RHINECANTHUS RECTANGULUS

Humuhumunukunukuapuaʻa

What a beautiful, lyrical, tongue-tiring, authentically Hawaiʻian name! As so often happens when I hear the mellifluous Hawaiʻian language spoken aloud in names like this, I also hear the unmistakable rhythm of ocean waves. Like other Hawaiʻian names – such as Haleakalā, the massive volcano on Maui, or Kalalau, my favourite trail on the coast of Kauai – it seems more like song than speech, more like water than words.

This particular name belongs to a marvellously colourful fish in the region. As the official Hawaiʻian state fish, humuhumunukunukuapuaʻa, also called the reef triggerfish, is familiar to generations of Hawaiʻians. That long, lovely name has an unexpected meaning – 'fish with the snout of a pig'.

1852 | David Starr Jordan | *Rhinecanthus rectangulus*

A special note for those who enjoy the Hawaiʻian language as much as I do: although the name of this fish is certainly long, it's actually not the longest word in Hawaiʻian. That honour is reserved for yet another fish, the lauwiliwilinukunukuʻoiʻoi, which means 'fish with a long snout shaped like a wiliwili leaf'.

In traditional Hawaiʻian lore, the humuhumunukunukuapuaʻa carries a lot of significance. For this fish symbolises Kamapuaʻa, the Hawaiʻian pig deity who represents fertility and is linked to the god of agriculture. Unfortunately, Kamapuaʻa has a violent, unpredictable personality. So his adventures aren't limited to agriculture. He famously shared a romantic relationship with Pele, the fire goddess. (Evidently, he found her pretty hot.) Legends tell of how he helped to transform the hard rock from Pele's lava into soft, productive soil. Even so, their time together was not exactly peaceful. They had many fierce battles with each other. As a result, you could describe their relationship as, well, volcanic.

TUBIPORA MUSICA

Organ Pipe Coral

Among the many colourful corals in the Indian and Pacific Oceans, organ pipe corals are especially beautiful. Like all corals, they are formed by colonies of tiny invertebrates related to jellies and sea anemones. And those colonies can move in unison if they are disturbed, retracting from any sources of danger. This particular variety of coral got its English name because the colonies create fused skeletons filled with parallel tubes that look a lot like organ pipes. Similarly, the Chinese name for this coral, *sheng shanhu*, was inspired by its resemblance to a traditional musical instrument made of vertical pipes.

c. 1800 | Friedrich Justin Bertuch | *Tubipora musica*

The scientific name, *Tubipora musica*, Latin for 'pipe music', echoes that imagery. Some scientists go further and attribute the term *musica* to the sound of seawater moving through the pipes. Imagine what a powerful musical experience it would be to hear that sound of the sea, with all its variations, playing throughout the oceans of the world – to hear the crescendos of currents and the rhythms of tides, the gentle waves and the raging storms, the flow and depth of timbres and dynamics in so many marvellous places.

Shapely and colourful as they are, with elegant forms and deep red hues, organ pipe corals are highly prized. Which is a problem, because they are now threatened by overzealous collectors as well as the warming of the oceans. Together, those two factors have caused populations to decline sharply. It's estimated that more than half of the world's organ pipe formations have disappeared in the past two decades.

But there is still hope: Dedicated conservationists and visionary governments have joined together to invest significantly in the protection of coral reefs. That investment will also support local economies, healthy oceans and the deep joy of knowing we can continue to live alongside these lovely creatures.

THECOSOMATA

Sea Butterfly

This delicate little creature, a small mollusc, is widely dispersed through the world's oceans, both north and south of the equator. The name is apt: sea butterflies have light, translucent shells and tiny wing-like arms that they use to propel themselves through the water, much like terrestrial butterflies do in the air.

Sea butterflies are exquisitely beautiful. Like their relatives that don't have shells, the sea angels, they are actually marine snails that have developed the ability to swim. They belong to the scientific order *Pteropoda* (meaning 'wing footed'), so called because their wings have evolved from the 'foot' common to all snails. In fact, the German name for them is *flügelschnecke*, meaning 'wing snails'. And thanks to those wings, sea butterflies have the ability to move freely in their marine environment.

They have also developed another special ability, one which helps them to find food. Sea butterflies can secrete mucous to produce small but effective nets that float in the seawater. When the microscopic organisms known as plankton drift too close, they are caught by these mucous nets. After enough time has passed, the nets fill up, and the sea butterflies can have a sumptuous plankton feast.

Scientists consider sea butterflies a helpful measure of climate change. Why? Because their shells are made from calcium carbonate, which grows scarcer as sea temperatures and acidity levels rise. That, in turn, harms their health and lowers their population, diminishing the biodiversity of the seas. As a result, the overall condition of sea butterflies can tell us much about the overall condition of our oceans. And because oceans comprise over 70 per cent of Earth's surface, if they are imperiled, then so are we, along with all the rest of our fellow creatures.

In this poignant way, a single, delicate creature, no bigger than one of your fingernails, shares a striking kinship with our home planet that supports all life.

NEOCLINUS BLANCHARDI

Sarcastic Fringehead

No kidding – that's the real English name of this fish.

Found in the saltwater shallows of North America's Pacific coast, sarcastic fringeheads have distended jaws that can expand enormously. Those huge mouths are filled with dangerously sharp teeth, which the fish use aggressively to attack any foes. If an intruder comes too close to a sarcastic fringehead's home, there's no defender more vicious, no fighter more ferocious.

What could possibly have inspired such a bizarre name for this creature? Well, the word 'fringehead' isn't difficult to explain, because it describes the loose, droopy growth on the fish's head. Honestly, it looks like a really bad haircut.

But what about 'sarcastic'? At first glance, that word seems to make no sense at all. Does this fish make tart, snarky comments to mock its fellow reef dwellers? Would it host a caustic, late-night talk show on the reef? As fun as that is to imagine – no.

The explanation lies in the word's intriguing etymology. Before the word 'sarcastic' took on its modern-day meaning, referring to sarcasm as a form of humour, it had a more physical meaning. It originally derived from *sarkázein*, a Greek verb meaning 'to rip apart flesh'. Thus, it could be used to describe a brutal attack against an enemy. Which is, of course, something that these highly volatile, battle-ready fish do with great gusto.

Yet that's not the end of the story. Word enthusiasts will note that there's still a close connection between the original Greek term and its modern descendant. While the early form describes a vicious attack at the physical level, tearing apart a person's body, the modern form describes an equally vicious attack at the psychological level, tearing apart a person's reputation, intelligence or ability. In one case, sharp teeth will cut deeply into someone's flesh; in the other case, sharp humour will cut deeply into someone's feelings.

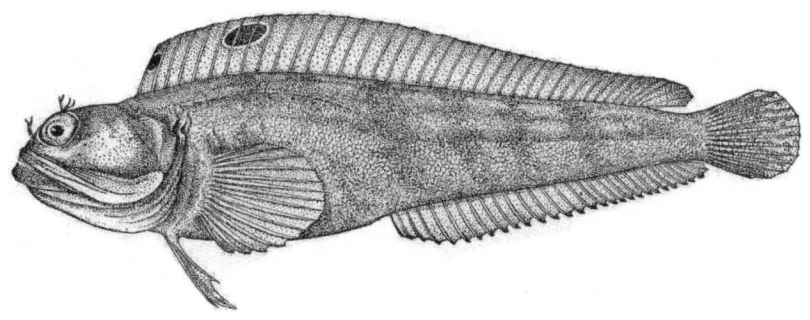

1907 | David Starr Jordan | *Neoclinus blanchardi*

An Encounter with a Whale

A briny breeze tousled my hair, waking me before dawn. Somewhere nearby, a seagull screeched. This was, I knew, my last day camping on the beach of Mexico's San Ignacio Lagoon. Shivering in the chilly air, I rubbed my hands together to warm them. A lone crab skittered past on the sand. For a moment I just stood there, looking out to sea. Slowly, the first golden rays of sunrise began to sparkle on the waves. As I scanned the bay, one question filled my mind. Would I see any whales?

Grey whales – once called 'devil fish' by North American hunters but now known for their peaceful curiosity about humans – normally migrated through these waters at this time of year. This was why I'd come. Yet I'd camped here for several days without spying a single one. And this morning was my last chance to see one of those magnificent creatures before returning home.

I pulled my kayak into the water, climbed inside, and started to drift into the darkened lagoon. Completely alone, I began to paddle. Ocean smells washed over me, and a tangle of kelp floated past. Gliding into the bay, I watched delicate threads of gold, peach and pink light start to shimmer on the waves. And I listened. To the gentle slap of waves against the bow. To the drip, drip, drip of water from the ends of my paddle. To the swelling calls of cormorants, pelicans and other waterbirds.

Further into the lagoon I paddled. As the sunlight grew stronger, I studied the wide span of water. No sign of whales anywhere. I sighed, increasingly sure that my dream was not going to be fulfilled.

All at once – a huge wave rose just ahead. A great flipper burst out of the water, then crashed down on the surface, soaking me with salty spray. An enormous head lifted higher, towering above my little boat.

Suddenly I was staring into the deepest, darkest eye that I'd ever seen. The eye of a grey whale.

For a timeless moment, we peered at each other. This whale, I knew, had migrated thousands of miles across open ocean to reach this place. What an immense journey! Then my admiration shifted to grief, for I recalled that my own kind had brutally hunted these whales to the very brink of extinction – and continues to threaten them today with illegal hunting, fishing net entanglements and pollution.

And yet . . . a new wave of feeling flowed through me, filling me like a swelling tide. Gratitude. For this whale and I were fellow living creatures. Fellow breathers of the air. Fellow mortals trying to make sense of our lives. Fellow sailors on the seas of this lonely planet. Peering into that deep, dark eye, I felt that all our differences – all the millions of years of evolutionary time that separated us – simply vanished. What mattered most was our deep similarity. Our shared mortality. Our parallel time on Earth. We were forever connected, this whale and I.

CHAPTER 3

Roots and Rainbows

I think that
I shall never see

A poem lovely
as a tree.

JOYCE KILMER, 'TREES'

ARETHUSA BULBOSA

Dragon's Mouth Orchid

With a luscious flower that is gorgeous pink, magenta and yellow, this orchid fairly shouts for attention from pollinators. 'Come closer and treat yourself to a feast!' it calls brazenly. Just to leave nothing to chance, it also has an alluring scent. On top of that, it displays ultraviolet bristles that add greater attraction for bees. And to make the invitation to visit truly irresistible, the flower opens up wide, like an enormous mouth – a dragon's mouth.

Unfortunately for those pollinators, it's all a ruse. Those that enter don't find much in the way of nectar to reward them for making the effort to visit. What they do find, however, is abundant pollen, which quickly covers them.

Found in marshes and meadows in Canada and the United States, the dragon's mouth orchid bears the scientific name *Arethusa bulbosa*. The term *bulbosa*, which means 'bulbous' in Latin, marks it as an orchid. (The word 'orchid', by the way, comes from the Greek word *orchis*, which means 'testicle', because many orchids have root tubers whose shape resembles those organs.)

Arethusa, the first part of the name, was inspired by the Greek myth of Arethusa, a river nymph who served in the entourage of the goddess Artemis. After the loyal, good-hearted Arethusa was seen bathing in a river by a lustful river god who then pursued her, Artemis intervened and saved the nymph by transforming her into a freshwater spring. Which is why these glorious flowers bearing her name are associated with lovely, spring-moistened meadows.

That connection to Greek mythology is reminiscent of another orchid, *Calypso bulbosa*. This beautiful pink and purple orchid, which lies hidden deep in the forests of North America, is named after Calypso, the legendary sea nymph of Homer's *Odyssey*.

1925 | Mary Vaux Walcott | *Arethusa bulbosa*

The secretive nymph preferred to remain hidden away on her remote island in the epic (so much so that her name in Greek actually means 'concealed'). Anyone lucky enough to find her was immediately struck by her beauty, which the legends say rivalled that of a glorious flower.

One of my all-time favourites, this wildflower is commonly called 'fairy slipper'. That rather whimsical common name is also a fitting description, because the flower really does look like an elegant, intricately designed slipper, just right to be worn by a fairy. If you're ever lucky enough to find one growing in a dark and secluded grove, it's a magical experience.

EUCALYPTUS DEGLUPTA

Rainbow Eucalyptus

Deep in the rainforests of Papua New Guinea, Indonesia and the Philippines lives the world's most colourful tree. The trunks of rainbow eucalyptus trees are striped with vibrant hues of purple, green, orange, red and brown. As the bark matures, strips peel off, revealing yet more bright colours. It's as if a tree and a painter's palette have merged into one. Whenever sunlight touches these trees, their trunks become as luminous and colourful as rainbows.

Among the tallest trees in the rainforest, reaching up to around 75 metres (250 feet), rainbow eucalyptus trees are integral to their ecosystems. Not only do they provide a habitat for many forest creatures, they are the food source for numerous species. And their roots give stability to the often steep terrain.

As with all kinds of eucalyptus, the leaves of these trees have a strong, resiny aroma that many believe helps to clear congestion. The smell is so distinctive, its source is instantly recognisable.

Like the fragrant balsam trees of eastern North America, or the sweet-smelling tepa trees cherished by the native Mapuche people of Patagonia, the smell of those leaves immediately calls to mind a particular kind of tree and its traditional habitat.

Rainbow eucalyptus trees are also revered in ancient cultures. Called *bagras* by Indigenous peoples in the Philippines, their leaves and bark are often used by traditional healers. Those leaves are useful in another way, too, because their smell helps to repel troublesome insects such as mosquitoes.

In addition, these trees provide inspiration for people everywhere, reminding us of nature's marvellous diversity of colour and design. They provide solace and insights for many, because their continual shedding of bark parallels the enduring human experience of loss, change and renewal. As one old layer dies and peels away, a new and vibrant layer that was hidden beneath is ultimately revealed.

Today, alas, these remarkable trees are seriously endangered by habitat loss from logging and agriculture. There is still enough time to save them through effective conservation measures. But that will only happen if enough courageous people choose to help them. If that happens, these trees could still have a bright and colourful future.

STRELITZIA REGINAE
Bird of Paradise Flower

Shaped like the plumed heads of brightly coloured birds, these flowers were named for their resemblance to the avian birds of paradise. Some ascribe the original name of those spectacular birds to a legend that they were simply so beautiful, so magnificent, they must have fallen to Earth from heaven itself.

'Paradise' as a word – as well as an enduring idea – appears in many of Europe's languages. In Germany, people speak of *paradies*; in France, *paradis*; in Spain and Portugal, *paraíso*; in Italy, *paradiso*. Those words came from the Latin *paradises*, which itself stemmed from the Greek *paradeisos*. What was the ultimate origin of the term? Most likely, it's the language of ancient Persia, whose word *pairi-daêzā* merged terms from Sanskrit and Ancient Greek to signify a special enclosure protected by an earthen wall. In other words – a garden.

Not surprisingly, these flowers have inspired other notable names. In South Africa, the only place where they're found in the wild today, people call them 'crane flowers' due to their similarity to crowned cranes. In fact, birds do have a special relationship to these flowers. Unlike the many plants that rely on insects for pollination, they have evolved to release their pollen onto the feet of birds that land on them. When those birds fly away, they carry that pollen to other flowers.

In 1788, the British botanist Joseph Banks gave an especially showy variety of the bird of paradise flower the name *Strelitzia regina*, in order to celebrate Queen Charlotte back in London. History buffs will know that she was the wife of King George III, who is remembered not as a flower but as a troubled man who suffered from mental illness, and as a monarch who oversaw the end of Britain's transatlantic slavery trade, the defeat of Napoleon at Waterloo and the loss of England's hold on some colonies in North America.

1807 | Sydenham Edwards | *Strelitzia reginae*

1887 | Walther Otto Müller | *Digitalis purpurea*

DIGITALIS PURPUREA

Foxglove

The flower we call 'foxglove' is strikingly beautiful, but that beauty isn't limited to just its appearance. With one of the most evocative names in nature, it invites us to imagine a fox adorning its paws with elegant, luxurious gloves. That very image has inspired many paintings, poems and songs, and has persisted for centuries. In fact, the ancient Anglo Saxon term for the flower was *foxes glofa*, which is often translated as 'glove of a fox'.

However, some linguists who have studied *foxes glofa* suggest that the word 'foxes' actually had a different original meaning – 'fairies' or 'the good folk'. Maybe the flowers weren't originally seen as gloves for foxes but rather as bonnets or gloves for the elusive Little People themselves.

Supporting this notion, the flower's Gaelic name, *lus nam ban-sith*, links the foxglove to 'the fairy woman'. Some people believe that the petals, when closely examined, show the fingerprints of these magical beings. Even today, some English people claim it's terribly bad luck to pick a foxglove. Why? Because that would incur the unending wrath of the fairy folk.

The roles of this plant in ancient lore don't end there, sprouting up like so many flowers in the fields. Celtic tales list foxglove as an essential ingredient in the potion that enables witches to fly, and tell of vengeful foxes wearing the flowers whenever they attacked village folk. Still others speak of the flower as a harmful source of poison (which is in fact true). Some of its nicknames, such as 'dead man's bells', testify to the potency of its toxins.

In one of nature's many surprising twists, those very same toxins are also a powerful source of healing. Herbalists discovered long ago that extracts from foxglove leaves could help to treat some heart ailments, such as poor circulation. During the First World War, British people collected foxgloves to be used as medicine for ailing soldiers. In more recent times, foxglove became the original source of the pharmaceutical drug digitalis, an important treatment for heart disease.

Whether it is helping witches fly, filling apothecary shelves, crowning the heads of fairies, curing heart problems or adorning well-dressed foxes – the possibilities, whether real or imagined, are endless. You could say, for this flower, striking beauty and unlimited possibilities go hand in glove.

IPOMOEA ALBA

Moonflower

This pure white flower blooms only at night, fully earning the 'moon' in its name. Much like the phases of the moon that go from the darkness of a new moon to the radiance of a full moon over the course of a lunar month, this flower has its own starkly different phases. During a single night, it will transform from no blossom at all into a completely formed flower. Then, by the first glimmer of sunrise, it will close up completely, ready to begin the cycle again the following night.

When it first blooms, a moonflower releases an alluring fragrance that attracts the highly elusive sphinx moth. The two species enjoy a symbiotic relationship; the moth pollinates the flower, while itself benefiting from its energy-rich nectar. Interestingly, there's a rare variation to the colour of these flowers. While most moonflowers are white, sometimes they can be deep blue or even purple. (Of course, that happens only once in a blue moon.)

1808 | William Curtis | *Ipomoea alba*

Also called 'moonvine' and 'sacred datura' by English-speaking admirers, this flower is found throughout the tropical and sub-tropical Americas, from Mexico to Argentina, as well as in parts of Arizona and Florida. Several millennia before Charles Goodyear invented a commercial process to produce rubber, ancient Mesoamerican people had already figured out how to mix this plant with material from the tree *Castilla elastica* to make balls that could actually bounce.

With its ethereal white blossom, moonflowers have inspired many other names, many of them reverential. To people in the Yucatán, it's called *oración*, meaning 'prayer', evoking deep devotion to God. In some parts of the Caribbean, it's dubbed 'the evening star'. In that same spirit, European botanists chose to call it *calonyction*, which is Greek for 'beauty of the night'.

However, as in all human affairs, there are differing points of view. People in Honduras have a less worshipful name for this flower: *pañal de niño*. That means, literally, 'child's nappy'.

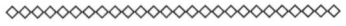

SEQUOIA SEMPERVIRENS

Sempervirens

'Always alive'. That's the meaning of *sempervirens*, the scientific name for the ancient evergreen trees that in English we commonly call coastal redwoods.

Those trees are named 'always alive' for good reason. For redwoods, time is measured not in minutes or hours, nor even in years, but in the cycle of centuries. They can grow to be more than two thousand years old.

To give that number some perspective, consider this: an elder redwood that's currently thriving was a sturdy young sapling when Jesus Christ walked in Galilee. It had already grown to an enormous height when Confucius taught philosophy in China. It was a mature adult by the time Joan of Arc rallied the people of France and Herr Gutenberg built his printing press in Germany. It was ancient but enduring when a young woman named Jane Goodall first travelled to Africa. And it's still standing strong today.

What's more, redwoods are the world's tallest trees, reaching up to 116 metres (380 feet) high. Held within their highest boughs are entire ecosystems of rare plants and animals, including birds that thrive in the uppermost canopies, salamanders that never leave the branches on which they are born and many unusual species of mosses, ferns and flowers. So sturdy are redwoods that their branches can actually support smaller trees, which plant themselves in those airy reaches.

Even the roots of these trees are remarkable, spreading out widely and weaving together with the roots of their neighbours. As a result, the trees in any grove will gain mutual support from each other. And when an elder finally falls, young redwoods will grow directly from its roots – the new generation rising from the fertile remains of the old. Found only in the hills and valleys of California's Pacific coast, ancient redwoods once covered more than 800,000 hectares (2 million acres). Today, after many years of aggressive logging, only about 5 per cent of that original forest still stands. Of those trees, just one quarter of the total has been protected for future generations.

The common name for these trees comes from the distinctive reddish colour of their wood. They have two impressive cousins – the giant sequoia, which is the most massive tree on the planet, and the dawn redwood, found in the Hubei province of China. Yet neither of those varieties stands nearly as tall as the towering redwoods of the California coast. How do they grow so amazingly tall? The secret lies in their ability to drink directly from the fog that rolls inland from the Pacific Ocean, bringing moisture to their upper boughs. So these trees can sustain their height without needing to draw water all the way up from their roots.

These majestic giants of the forest have long been revered by Native Americans. To the Yurok people, they are *keehl*, and are considered sacred. The Miwok, for their part, call the trees *woh-woh-nau*, imitating the call of an owl that always watches over them. One Yurok legend tells the creation story of Redwood, a being as old as time, who taught the first people how to build their canoes.

Anyone who walks among the sempervirens feels a profound sense of awe . . . as well as humility. These trees are true giants, pillars stretching from soil to sky. And their great power to inspire is, indeed, always alive.

DIONAEA MUSCIPULA

Venus Flytrap

Powerfully attractive but potentially fatal, this plant was named after Venus, the alluring Roman goddess of love. Her name is linked to such Latin words as *venerius*, meaning 'erotic'; *venerātiō*, meaning 'adoration'; and *venerari*, meaning 'to love deeply' or 'to revere'. It has also been suggested that the goddess could be etymologically connected with *venenum*, a term for deadly poisons as well as irresistible charms.

And this plant's mythical connections don't end there. The scientific name for its genus is *Dionaea* – a nod to Aphrodite, the Greek goddess of love, beauty and sexual attraction who was the precursor of Venus.

1786 | John Hill | *Dionaea muscipula*

Why all these associations with powerful desire? Because many insects and other small beings are lured, irresistibly and inexorably, into the jaw-like leaves of the Venus flytrap.

Growing wild in the marshes of southeastern United States, this carnivorous plant is, for its prey, almost impossible to escape. By the time any unfortunate fly, ant, beetle, slug or spider has entered the danger zone, its fate has most likely been sealed. For as soon as the plant's sensitive hairs detect any movement, the jaws clamp shut. No wonder the species name for this plant, *muscipula*, is simply the Latin for 'flytrap'.

Because the soil of its native marshes often lacks sufficient nutrients, the Venus flytrap needed to evolve some way to expand its diet. That required developing the abilities of a carnivore. Which is why the plant's very existence depends on being deeply attractive – as well as fatal – to its potential sources of nourishment.

Some folk who live close to its habitat use a different name for the plant, calling it 'tipitwitchet'. This name likely has Native American roots, coming from *titipiwitshik*, a Powhatan Renape term describing leaves that 'wind around' their prey, embracing tightly. For the unlucky insect that ventures too close, it's an embrace that's literally to die for.

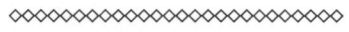

FITZROYA CUPRESSOIDES

Alerce

High in the rainforests of Patagonia grow some of the world's oldest living beings: alerce trees. They can grow to be more than two millennia old, and one in Argentina has been confirmed as more than 2,600 years old. Researchers recently located one that could be 5,000 years old, which means it might have

1851 | Walter Hood Fitch | *Fitzroya cupressoides*

sprouted before the Great Pyramid of Giza was even a gleam in the pharaoh's eye.

The alerce trees I saw recently in the Pucheguin region of Chile have been standing strong for many centuries, perhaps even since the last ice age. In addition to their longevity, their enormity is astounding. They stand as ancient guardians of the rainforest, with immense trunks, gnarled roots and powerful boughs.

Alerce is the Spanish name for these ancient conifers (which are related to pine trees even though they are deciduous and shed their leaves annually). The Indigenous Mapuche people have given them a different name, however. In their language, Mapudungun, these trees are called *lawal*, which is believed to be related to *lahuen*, the word for 'medicine'. Sure enough, the accuracy of that connection has been affirmed by recent scientific studies suggesting that these trees may help to treat skin wounds and other conditions such as psoriasis.

Yet I wonder whether that's the whole story. Could these magnificent trees also have a different sort of medicinal value? Might they hold the power to help conditions that aren't just physical – conditions that are, instead, emotional or spiritual? In the beloved Japanese tradition of 'forest bathing', being fully present with trees opens all of our senses, immersing us in the colours, aromas, sounds, textures and tastes of these beings. The experience deepens our awareness both inside and outside ourselves, connecting us to life's most enduring qualities, values and blessings.

Perhaps, in a similar way, the Mapuche people have long understood that simply being in the presence of these ancient trees could help to heal the human soul.

PEDICULARIS GROENLANDICA

Elephant Head Flower

Every summer, in the alpine meadows near my home in Colorado, I find many magnificent wildflowers. They display a dazzling array of colours, aromas and designs. Growing in the mountains at elevations up to 3,800 metres (12,500 feet), they may appear rather delicate – but they are, in fact, amazingly hardy, strong enough to survive the extreme temperatures and storms of the high country.

One of the most improbable types of wildflowers is also one of my favourites, with blossoms that look strikingly like the heads of pink and purple elephants. Yes, it's true – elephants. Complete with broad ears and curly trunks. It's no surprise they are commonly called 'elephant heads' or 'elephantella'. Whenever I find them growing in clusters beside streams or melting snow, they remind me of herds of miniature elephants gathered at their favourite watering holes.

Oddly enough, the scientific genus to which these flowers belong is *Pedicularis*, which is related to the Latin name for an entirely different form of life – the pesky little beings commonly called 'lice'. (That name, by the way, is the plural; the singular is 'louse', which is the root of the adjective 'lousy'.) What does this beautiful Rocky Mountain flower have to do with lice? Absolutely nothing – except for the fact that there was an old superstition that if cattle ate these plants, they would attract lice. Although that erroneous belief was dispelled long ago, many people continued to call the plants of this genus 'lousewort'. That's a very unfortunate label for these wonderful flowers, a twist of naming that's just plain lousy.

1925 | Mary Vaux Walcott | *Pedicularis groenlandica*

Native Americans have long used these plants for medicinal purposes. Blackfoot people prize them for reducing inflammation and pain. Cheyenne grind the stems and leaves into powder and make a drink that may ease coughing. Ojibwa, for their part, view these plants as an aphrodisiac.

Herbalists outside of these tribes also value the plants of this genus as mild sedatives or as treatments to help relax muscles. Some burn them to encourage better sleep. Some believe the plants have hallucinogenic properties. And some, I'm sure, simply enjoy them for their whimsical beauty that inspires thoughts of elephants.

PLAGIOMNIUM CUSPIDATUM

Baby Tooth Moss

Named for the tiny teeth along the edges of its leaves, baby tooth moss grows in the forests of North America, Europe, Africa and parts of Asia. It's used by birds (as well as other creatures such as salamanders) for making their comfy nests. And it may have valuable medicinal uses due to its ability to deter microbial pathogens.

In Britain, this plant has an adorably natural name: 'woodsy thyme-moss'. Now, it's easy to explain why the word 'woodsy' was included in that label. As well as 'moss', since it is a variety of moss. But why 'thyme'? Most likely, people noticed how much the pointed leaves of the moss resemble those of the fragrant herb. So British chefs of language simply decided to add a pinch of thyme to the recipe.

The word 'moss' has a long and complex history. It has spread like, well, a certain type of green plant, flourishing in the rich terrains of many different languages. Beginning with the

Proto-Indo-European *meus*, which referred to damp places like swamps and bogs as well as the vegetation found there, the word evolved into the Latin word *muscus*, and eventually *mossa*. From there, it moved into German as *mios*. Over time, in the highly unpredictable ways of language, it spread into other tongues, including Slavonic (*muchu*), Hungarian (*moha*), Norse (*mosi*), Italian (*muschio*), Old English (*meos*), Lithuanian (*mūsai*), Spanish (*musgo*) and Danish (*mos*). As well as the French term for moss (*mousse*) – which is not to be confused with the name of a certain delectable dessert.

Which leads us to the famous proverb 'A rolling stone gathers no moss'. That maxim has travelled its own unpredictable path. It first appeared more than two thousand years ago in a passage usually attributed to the Latin writer Publilius Syrus. But it wasn't until Erasmus restated it five hundred years later, in a work that waited another thousand years to be translated into English, that the proverb became well known. Since then, portions have been adapted or referenced by writers as different as J. R. R. Tolkien, O. Henry and Ken Kesey, as well as countless songwriters, artists, speakers and poets. And let's not forget that it also inspired the name of a certain rock band featuring Mick Jagger.

ADIANTUM CAPILLUS-VENERIS
Maidenhair Fern

Across Europe, the Americas, Africa and many parts of Asia, people have long appreciated maidenhair fern. In addition to its symmetrical beauty, the fern's thin stalks resemble human hair. Moreover, its fronds are able to shed water while remaining dry regardless of whether the water comes from a torrential rain or a single drop of dew.

These qualities, put together, led to an association with Venus, the Roman goddess of love. For in mythology, Venus was born fully grown from the ocean, with hair that was long and flowing, yet completely dry. Hence early observers called the plant *capillaris veneris*, or 'hair of Venus'. And its scientific genus name, *Adiantum*, arose from *adiantos*, the Greek word for 'not wetted'.

Over two thousand years ago, Pliny the Elder observed that this plant was commonly called 'beautiful hair'. He also noted the irony that maidenhair fern often grows in very wet places, yet it repels any moisture. What scientists have discovered recently is that the ferns shed water in order to protect themselves from harmful bacteria and any materials that could interfere with photosynthesis. This helpful ability to cleanse itself, known as superhydrophobia, is commonly called 'the lotus effect' because it's also characteristic of lotus flowers.

Now, about that resemblance to human hair. As we know, the truth can sometimes morph into legend and unfounded superstitions. Because the delicate leaf stalks look so much like hair, people conjectured that maidenhair fern could actually be used to cure baldness. Salesmen were happy to satisfy the, ahem, growing demand. So in the nineteenth century, men all across Europe enthusiastically rubbed maidenhair elixir on their scalps. Alas, the gap between expectations and reality was much bigger than a hairsbreadth.

Maidenhair fern has also inspired other legends, mainly due to its association with innocence and purity. That's why, in Appalachian folklore, it is said that only someone who is truly pure of heart can hold a maidenhair fern without making any of its leaves tremble.

That's not the only example of ferns inspiring legends. Puzzled by the fact that ferns seemed to appear out of nowhere, as if by magic, many people across medieval Europe speculated that ferns had invisible seeds – and could actually make people invisible. (Because the microscope hadn't yet been invented, people didn't know about ferns' tiny spores that spread like dust particles.)

As a result, ferns were prized as talismans to protect against evil or to confer invisibility. And so, for centuries, shepherds in Normandy used ferns to guard their flocks against attacks from evil beings. Meanwhile, Slavic swimmers wove ferns into their hair to avoid drowning. A story written around two hundred years ago by Hans Christian Andersen, 'The Travelling Companion', describes ferns with such magical powers.

My favourite legend about ferns comes from Baltic folklore. Tales are told of a uniquely magical fern that blooms only once, on Midsummer Eve. It flowers beautifully for a brief instant, radiant in the night – then disappears completely. Nothing remains, not even a single drop of dew.

c. **1880** | James Britten | *Adiantum capillus-veneris*

c. 1910 | Charles Flahault | *Parnassia palustris*

PARNASSIA PALUSTRIS
Grass of Parnassus

Mount Parnassus has a truly prominent place in Greek mythology. Sacred to the gods Apollo and Dionysus, this mountain was also the home of the Muses, nine sublime goddesses who inspired the epic poetry, literature, music, dance and science of ancient Greece. The ancient oracle of Delphi lies on the mountain's lower flank – which was the spot where, in one famous myth, Apollo finally slayed the dragon Python. Here, too, was the home of Pegasus, the great flying horse ridden by Bellerophon (who attained glory by defeating the monstrous Chimera). And somewhere hidden among its crags was the Corycian Cave of Pan, the wild god of nature.

According to legend, the mountain got its name from Parnassos, a survivor of a flooded settlement who made his home somewhere on the sacred mountain. Later, when people found a lovely star-shaped flower growing on those grassy slopes, they chose to call it 'grass of Parnassus', a name that linked the flower to the pantheon of Greek gods. No doubt some imagined that Pegasus himself, roaming long ago on that same mountainside, had grazed on those very blossoms.

The flower also grows in many places far from Greece. These include places as diverse as the wetlands of southern Appalachia, the tundra of Alaska and the English county of Cumberland. That county, in fact, takes such great pride in the plant that grass of Parnassus is its official flower.

In some places, however, the flower is called simply 'bog star'. While that's somewhat descriptive, it's a far less glorious name than one that refers to Parnassus, home to all those powerful gods and creatures. Most likely, Pegasus would not approve.

PERSICARIA ORIENTALIS

Kiss-Me-Over-the-Garden-Gate

With such a romantic name, you'd expect this plant to be lush and beautiful. And so it is. Growing tall and elegant, with deep pink bunches of flowers, it has dangled gracefully over garden gates in many lands, from Australia to Europe to North America.

While travelling in the region of the Black Sea over three centuries ago, the French botanist Joseph Pitton de Tournefort spotted these flowers near Tbilisi, Georgia, and on Mount Ararat in eastern Turkey. With the help of a Capuchin friar, he obtained the seeds. A full-blown romance with this lovely plant soon swept across Europe.

Although it was highly prized by gardeners in the Victorian era, the alluringly named kiss-me-over-the-garden-gate fell gradually out of favour a century ago, being viewed as somewhat old-fashioned. But it has regained popularity in recent years, especially among people who grow the most cherished heirloom varieties. So the plant is again adorning the garden gates of folk who appreciate its rosy blossoms – and, of course, the romantic kisses those blossoms might inspire.

Like other flowers that have ebbed and flowed in popularity over time, this one has several different names. It's also called 'ladyfinger', 'prince's feather', 'Oriental persicary' and even 'ragged sailor'. To my mind, though, none of those has nearly as much whimsy and charm as kiss-me-over-the-garden-gate.

Worth noting is the botanical fact that the seeds of this plant need to experience the cold, harsh temperatures of winter before they can germinate in the warm, welcoming days of spring. So they must suffer and struggle before they can ultimately thrive and bloom. Hmmmm . . . might that also be a metaphor for a good romance?

1792 | William Curtis | *Persicaria orientalis*

An Encounter with an Ancient Redwood Tree

Ambling beside a tumbling stream in Northern California, I entered a grove of redwoods.

What struck me first was the deepening quiet, which embraced those trees even as the morning mist embraced their branches. All I could hear was the crackle of my footsteps on fallen needles, the occasional sweep of birds' wings overhead and the splashes of the stream. And beneath all of that... a kind of quiet that wasn't merely the absence of sound but a deeper form of presence – the swelling silence of those great trees.

Then I saw one especially magnificent redwood. Its upper reaches towered above the rest of the grove, its boughs reaching high into the sky; the contours of its bark were so deeply carved, they looked like river canyons.

I decided then and there to stay with the ancient tree as long as possible. Though I didn't have a sleeping bag or food, I nestled myself among the great tree's roots, leaned back against its towering trunk and settled in for the night.

For a long time, I opened myself to my surroundings, doing my best to quiet my mind and resist the temptation of thinking too much.

With time, I began to feel just a hint of what it might be like to be a tree. How might it feel to stop running around, always moving in my human body and mind? I wondered what it would be like, instead, to stand tall, rooted deeply in a single place. To be completely present, wholly centred and fully alive. To feel content beyond human experience. To observe and communicate ceaselessly with the land, the weather, the creatures all around. For endless springs, summers, autumns and winters. Season after season, year after year, century after century.

Yet even as I sensed the vast lifespan of the tree, I knew that we weren't so different after all. Both of us were mortal, both alive for this instant in the grand sweep of cosmic time. I could almost hear the tree saying: 'I am not so young as you, perhaps. But old I surely am not. The mountains, they are old. The oceans, they are old. The sun is older still, as are the stars. And how old is the cloud, whose body is made from the vapours of an earlier cloud that once watered the soil, then flowed to the river, then rose again into the sky? I am part of the very first seed, planted in the light of the earliest dawn. And so are you. So perhaps we are neither older nor younger but truly the same age.'

All through the night, I stayed close to that tree, feeling its presence, breathing its air, sensing its wisdom. Though I don't remember sleeping at all, I do remember feeling fully alive and deeply at peace.

CHAPTER 4

Inspiring Insects

In the dry summer
field at nightfall,

fireflies rise
like sparks.

Imagine the
presence of ghosts

flickering

MARILYN KALLET, 'FIREFLIES'

ANISOPTERA

Dragonfly

Just think about the English name for this magnificent creature – and you know right away that it's part dragon, part fly. And also part miracle.

Even though it's no bigger than your hand, one of these extraordinary creatures can fly like a dragon of legend. It can swoop, hover, fly backwards, rise straight up and roll over – all while zipping swiftly through the air. No wonder people have appreciated dragonflies for a very long time. The first use of the word 'dragonfly' in a publication was well over three centuries ago, in 1667, by the British scientist Francis Bacon.

The dragonfly's beautiful, iridescent wings have caught the attention – and won the admiration – of people around the globe. They have inspired names like 'ebony jewelwing', which belongs to a species in North America. Or the whimsical label 'waterbutterfly', used for centuries in English folklore. Or the evocative Croatian name, *vilin konjic*, which means 'fairy horse'.

Those rapidly moving double wings also inspired the French name *libellule* – one of those words that's truly lovely to say aloud. That name, in fact, came from the Latin term *libellula*, meaning 'little book'. As the dragonfly's wings whir speedily, they sound like the pages of a book turning. What wonderful stories might those pages hold?

For centuries, people have conferred many other names on these little creatures (of which there are more than three thousand different kinds). Some, like 'mosquito hawks', 'blue dashers', 'banded darters', 'flame skimmers' and 'unicorn clubtails', show genuine appreciation. But not all names for dragonflies are so positive.

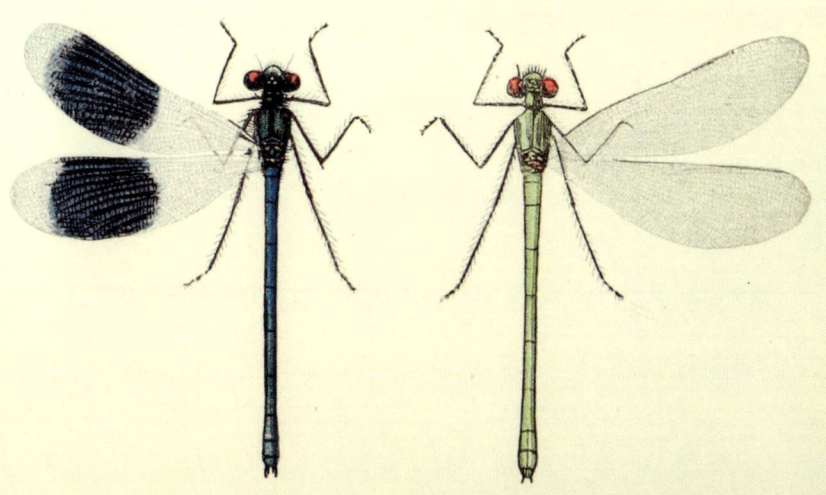

1900 | William John Lucas | *Anisoptera*

In medieval times, for instance, people called these insects 'devil's darning needles' because of the superstition that the devil could use them to sew a child's mouth completely shut or poke out someone's eyes so they would go blind. That notion led to pejorative names including 'eye snatchers', 'eye pokers' and 'hobgoblin flies'. Other superstitions linked dragonflies to deadly snakes, which caused some people to label them 'adder bolts' and 'snake doctors'. In Gaelic, they were called *tarbh-nathair-neimh*, which meant 'venomous bull serpents'.

Dragonflies have been on Earth significantly longer than humans. Fossils of the most ancient ones, called *Meganeuropsis*, are from the Permian period nearly 300 million years ago. Those early dragonflies were impressive beings, but believe me, you really wouldn't have wanted to have one buzzing around your head, for they were truly gigantic, each one the size of a hawk, with a wingspan of 75 centimetres (30 inches), about as long as your arm. Soaring over what is now western Europe, the United States and China, they were frightful and deadly predators. Fortunately for us, their modern descendants are a whole lot smaller.

For the Zuni people, a Native American tribe whose people have long lived on lands that are now the southwestern United States, dragonflies are beloved creatures. The Zunis have a lovely name for them: *shumak'olo:wa*. In Zuni lore, dragonflies are sacred messengers that have the great ability to travel to and from the spirit world. And they play an important and cherished role in this world, too. A Zuni friend once told me that he was taught this beautiful saying as a child: 'Where there are dragonflies, there is water, and where there is water, there is life.'

CHRYSIRIDIA RHIPHEUS
Madagascan Sunset Moth

The island of Madagascar, off the southeast coast of Africa, is truly a world apart. Known to the Greeks as Malai Gesira, its name evolved over time to the one we use today. Because it's been isolated for ages – having broken off from Africa almost 200 million years ago – its flora and fauna have evolved independently. As a result, it's a biodiversity haven, with over 90 per cent of its wildlife endemic to the island.

Madagascar overflows with treasures – enormous baobab trees, rich cultural traditions, beautiful orchids, diverse lemurs, hidden pirate coves and even a dramatic stone forest. Yet one of Madagascar's most glorious treasures is smaller than the palm of your hand – a moth with wings as colourful as a blazing sunset over the Indian Ocean.

The iridescent wings of the Madagascan sunset moth, which reflect light through complex arrays of tiny curved and layered scales, are constantly aglow. To see one of these moths in flight is to watch a fire coal on the wing; to see hundreds of them settle on the same bush is to watch those coals suddenly burst into flames.

In the ancient Malagasy tongue, the moth's names, *lolonandriana* and *adriandolo*, are packed with meaning. *Lolo* means 'spirit' as well as 'butterfly'. Meanwhile, *andriana* means 'kingly' and 'noble'. And these creatures truly deserve to be called 'kingly butterfly' or 'noble spirit', for they do indeed resemble the lavishly dressed emissaries of royal realm, a realm where light and colour reign supreme.

While most moths are nocturnal, moving around at night when there's less risk of predation from birds, this variety of moth prefers to be active throughout the day. Perhaps the moths' radiant wings scare off predators by signalling toxicity. Or could it be that these colourful moths just can't resist the opportunity to shimmer and shine bright?

1829 | William Swainson | *Chrysiridia rhipheus*

In fact, some Malagasy people regard moths and butterflies as the reincarnated souls of departed loved ones. Those souls have returned to join us on our own journey through mortality. It's wise not to harm them, because to hurt one of these winged creatures is really to attack someone's revered ancestor. Not a good idea for harmony – in this realm or any other.

STENOCARA GRACILIPES

Namib Desert Beetle

How would you find enough water to survive if you lived in one of the world's driest places? That's a very important question, and a truly existential challenge, for the beetles of Africa's Namib Desert.

The word Namib originated in the language of the Indigenous Khoi people. Its meaning? 'A vast place'. This enormous, windswept stretch of dunes surely is vast. But that's just part of what makes it so difficult to live there. It's also the oldest desert on Earth, having been dry for more than 50 million years – and it is, indeed, extremely dry. For this desert gets less than 1 centimetre (½ inch) of rain each year.

Faced with such a parched environment, Namib Desert beetles have found a unique solution to the problem of how to keep themselves hydrated and healthy. By climbing to the tops of dunes and lifting their forewings, which are covered with microscopic bumps and channels, these beetles use their own bodies to collect scarce water vapour directly from the air. The process, called 'fog basking', is so effective that it has enabled them to survive in the harshest of conditions.

On top of that, the ingenuity of these insects has prompted people to design a host of biomimicry inventions to harvest airborne water vapour. Those inventions – inspired by a bunch of small beetles in a remote desert – include irrigation technology, roof tiles that capture moisture and even water bottles that refill themselves.

While people often quote the proverb (which dates back to Plato) 'Necessity is the mother of invention', I beg to differ. Nature, really, is the mother of invention. That is a marvellous invitation to observe nature closely, a humbling reminder of how little we really know about the natural world and an important challenge to protect nature in every possible way.

The Namibian name for these beetles, *toktokkie*, comes from the sound they make by knocking their undersides against the sand. That drumming acts as a rhythmic love song, and it seems to work well enough to attract mates. (Which is, of course, the other truly existential challenge for these creatures.)

Besides, for those beetles, it must be nice to have some company up there on the dunes. Why fog-bask alone, if you can do it with a friend?

MORPHO HELENOR

Morpho Butterfly

Exquisitely beautiful, the radiant wings of morpho butterflies grace rainforests across South America, Central America and the Caribbean. There are twenty-nine species in total, all of them gorgeous, with around half of them found in the Ecuadorian Amazon.

The bright, metallic colours of morphos' wings aren't from pigments but from intricate microscopic scales that magnify and reflect certain wavelengths, creating luminous colours.

c. 1840 | Georges Cuvier | *Morpho helenor*

Whenever sunlight touches those wings, they light up brilliantly. As a result, these butterflies can be seen from great distances – up to 1 kilometre (two thirds of a mile) away. When viewed from different angles, the colours of the wings shift dramatically, moving from blue to green, lavender and purple.

Morpho is an Ancient Greek word with two meanings. It can describe something beautiful and appealing as well as something varied and changeable. The word is often associated with Aphrodite, the goddess of beauty, love and sexual desire. (There was even a cult, based in Corinth, devoted to a version of the goddess called Aphrodite Morpho.) The first person to use the name 'morpho butterfly', Johan Christian Fabricius, a Danish scientist in the eighteenth century, probably drew from both meanings, for he chose a term that celebrates the radiant beauty of these creatures as well as the changeable colours of their wings.

Habitat destruction and the fragmentation of tropical forests are the greatest threats to morphos today. Throughout their range, they are increasingly endangered by the loss of intact forest ecosystems. Yet despite these challenges, they continue, at least for now, to brighten our world.

Wonderful words for 'butterfly' float to our ears from many languages around the world. In French, the name is *papillon*, which evolved from ancient Indo-European words meaning 'to tremble or shake' (as the wings of butterflies do so delicately). In German, the name *schmetterling* originated with the Slavic word for cream – so in a lovely confluence of languages, German speakers make a connection with cream, while English speakers make a connection with butter. *Mariposa*, the Spanish name, probably stems from the Virgin Mary, and the spiritual idea that butterflies are the embodiments of human souls. By contrast, the Russian name, *babochka*, carries a darker meaning, linked to frightful dangers. It evolved from *baba*, the term in folklore for an old woman who just might actually be a witch.

That's only the beginning of the marvellous names for these equally marvellous creatures. In Italian, butterflies are called *farfalla*; in Balinese, *kupu-kupu*; and in Norwegian, *sommerfugl*. Portuguese speakers say *borboleta*; people in the Philippines favour *paruparo*; while many Chinese say *húdié* (蝴蝶). Hawaiʻians, whose native language is ever musical, say *pulelehua*. Swahili people use the word *kipepeo*. And in India, speakers of Hindi say *titlī* (तितली). In Welsh, butterflies are known as *pilipala*; in Dutch, *vlinder*; in Japanese, *chō* (蝶); and in Finnish, *perhonen*. And pretty much everywhere, they are called 'beautiful'.

While we're talking about these creatures . . . there's one more figure from Greek myth who deserves to be mentioned – Psyche, the goddess of the human soul. (Her name, of course, is the root for words such as 'psychology' and 'psychic'.) Her story, one of the most poignant tales ever told, describes how she endured terrible loss and hardship before, at last, reuniting with her lover and ultimately gaining immortality. It's a story of immense suffering, devotion and, finally, renewal. That's why Psyche is revered as an example of the enduring strength of love, the soul's connection with the divine and the power of transformation.

And what is Psyche's symbol? A butterfly.

LAMPYRIDAE

Firefly

Wherever fireflies appear, they evoke wonder ... and perhaps a glimpse of the mysteries beyond our mortal world. For example, Japanese legends maintain that two kinds of fireflies, *heike-botaru* and *genji-botaru*, are actually the ghosts of fallen warriors. Meanwhile, on the other side of the world, Indigenous Amazonian traditions see the light of fireflies as a gift from the gods.

For Native Americans, fireflies have been equally inspiring. Cherokees call them *ulikèdvsï*, meaning 'little sparks', and consider them the spirits of deceased ancestors. To the Ojibwe people, fireflies are *bebiguwiishkaanan*, 'little fire beings', and are believed to hold enduring powers of safety and health. For the Navajos, fireflies are guardians of the world's eternal qualities, including beauty and balance.

One of my favourite kinds of firefly, the 'blue ghost', is found in the southern Appalachian Mountains. Unlike many species, blue ghosts blaze with a steady light rather than a flashing pattern. Some say their ethereal glow, often seen floating through fields and forests, is really the light of departed souls.

The first known use of the English name 'firefly' was in 1598, when a teacher, John Florio, combined the word 'fire' and 'fly'. Over time, these radiant insects have garnered many other evocative English names, including 'lightning bugs', 'candleflies', 'firebobs', 'glowworms' and 'lamp bugs'. But my personal choice for the most mellifluous name is 'will-o-the-wisps'. While that term is most often used to describe the spooky flames from the gases of decaying plants in marshes (also sometimes called *ignis fatuus*, Latin for 'foolish fire'), it's also sometimes a colloquial term for fireflies. However it's used, something about that name stirs a subtle breeze in my mind.

I can almost hear the summer wind swishing through the grasses, almost see those little lights glittering all around.

The ancient Greeks, too, appreciated fireflies, associating their light with beneficial guidance, courage and hope. Although fireflies don't appear in any of the most famous Greek myths, they do add sparkle to folklore and songs. Not surprisingly, the Greeks had their own name for these beetles with glowing tails. They called fireflies *kysolampis*, which merged two words – *kysos* (buttocks) and *lampein* (to shine).

Whatever you may choose to call these creatures, it's safe to conclude this: as long as fireflies keep illuminating the night, people everywhere will keep celebrating them.

ACTIAS LUNA

Luna Moth

The luna moth's eerie green wings, with feather-like extensions and prominent eye markings, make any sighting surprising as well as magical. Also called the 'moon moth', it can be found on spring evenings across much of eastern North America.

'Motions of the moon'. That's the literal meaning of the moth's scientific name, *Actias luna*. Conferred over two centuries ago by the Swedish biologist Carl Linnaeus, the name was inspired by the mythology of Luna, the Roman goddess of the moon. The reference to the goddess was originally prompted by those eye markings that adorn the luna's wings, because they also resemble crescent moons. And the reference is fitting for another reason, as well – the moth's elegant, ethereal appearance seems as lovely as the moon's glow.

Like the phases of the moon, the life of this moth passes quickly; an adult will live for only nine or ten days. And because it doesn't have a mouth, nor the ability to digest food, the luna moth never eats. Instead, after emerging from its silken cocoon called a pupa, it relies on the fat supply it stored away as a caterpillar. That's enough to give it the energy needed for flying, mating and occasionally dazzling humans.

The traditions of some Native American tribes consider the luna moth a sign of spiritual support and guidance. Cherokees, for example, tell tales of how this creature brought the light of the moon into our world, revealing darkened paths and providing new hope. The moth also inspires other, non-Indigenous peoples in North America. Many of them celebrate the moth's mystical appeal, especially its connection to divine femininity and the eternal spirit.

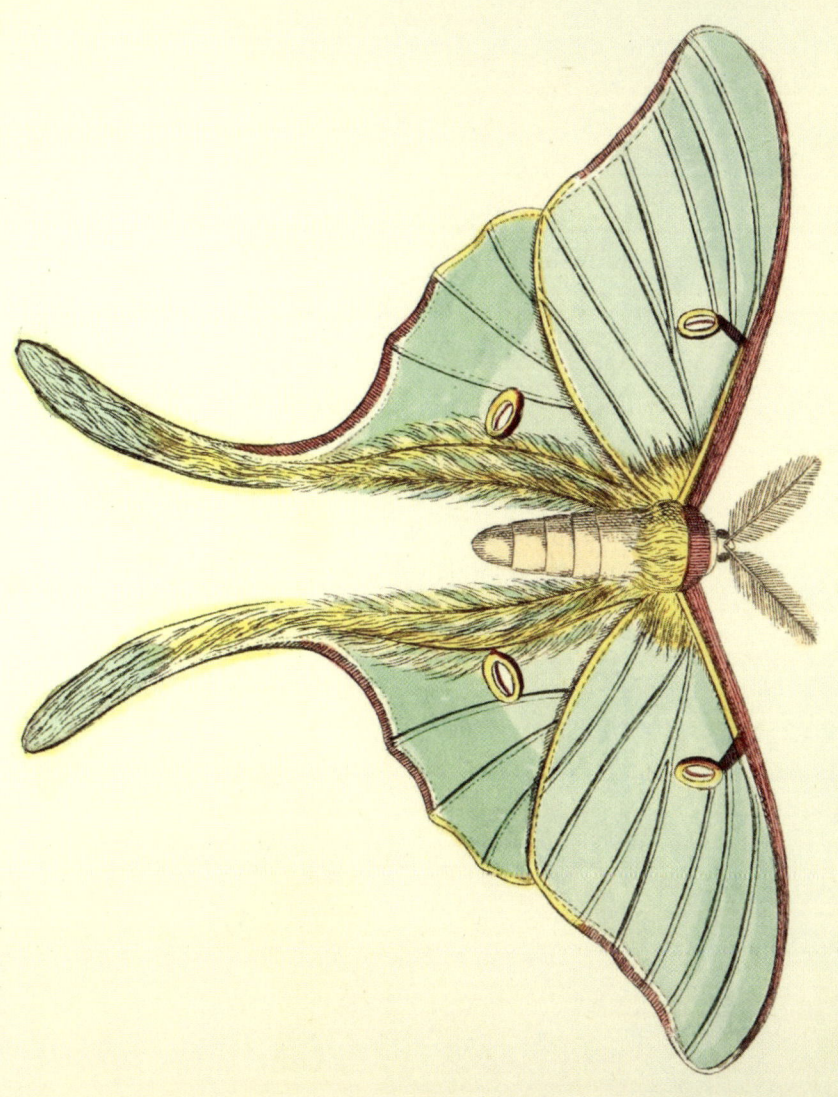

c. 1780 | Georg Heinrich von Borowski | *Actias luna*

Meanwhile, the moth's close relative, the Asian moon moth, ranges across India, China, Malaysia, Korea and Japan. Equally wondrous and slightly bluer in colour, its evocative Japanese name, *ōmizuao*, means 'blue waters'. In Chinese folklore, this moth represents immortality and is often depicted with the deity Xiwangmu, the goddess who oversees the transition of souls to the afterlife. Whenever a moon moth appears during the Chinese mid-autumn festival, it's taken as a positive and auspicious sign, the harbinger of a good year to come.

MANTODEA

Praying Mantis

Not surprisingly, the praying mantis is named for its appearance as someone in a prayerful stance. In fact, 'mantis' is derived from the Greek term *mantikos* (μαντικός), which means 'like an oracle', 'seer' or 'prophet'.

This insect is also unusual for its triangular head, which can swivel in many directions. In fact, the mantis is capable of turning its head 180 degrees (something no other insect can do). This capability helps it to spot potential prey with its compound eyes, which provide excellent, three-dimensional vision.

Yet it's the evocative posture of this insect that has made it so famous. For centuries, it's been admired by diverse cultures around the world. And the extent of that admiration is simply astounding.

In China, the insect's deliberate, stealthy and focused movements helped to inspire the founding 1,500 years ago of Shaolin kung fu, considered by many to be the original form of martial arts. Japanese culture has long valued the insect as an unstoppable warrior. And in ancient Egypt, the mantis represented a guide for people in their greatest quests. For generations of Celts, the insect's posture signified deep devotion and perseverance in the face of hardship. Meanwhile, Native Americans have long revered the insect as a symbol of the Great Spirit and the enduring continuity of life.

Names for the praying mantis in many languages convey that same sense of reverence. The Russian name, *bogomolka* (Богомолка), translates as 'she who prays to God', while the German name, *Gottesanbeterin*, means 'God worshipper'. That's very similar to the Portuguese, *louva-a-deus*, 'God praiser'. The name in Afrikaans, *bidsprinkhaan*, has a similar meaning – the word *bid* means 'to pray', while *sprinkhaan* means 'grasshopper'.

1921 | Edward Julius Detmold | *Mantodea*

In the same vein, the French call this insect *mante religieuse*, meaning 'religious mantis', while speakers of Persian say *âxundak*, which translates as 'little cleric' (آخوندک).

These religious associations sometimes take a different twist, imagining the mantis as a miniature steed. For example, the name in modern Greek, *aloyaki tis Panagias* (αλογάκι της Παναγίας), means 'the little horse of the Mother of Jesus'. In the West Indies, people also call this insect 'God horse', while the Turkish name, *peygamberdevesi*, means 'the prophet's camel'.

Among all these delightful names for the praying mantis, my favourite is the one from Hungary. To the Hungarians, it's called *ájtatos manó*. Which means, literally, 'pious pixie'. Appropriately, the scientific name for this celebrated creature is *Mantis religiosa*, which is Latin for 'religious mantis'. That name, as we know, reflects an entire world of devotion.

An Encounter with a Luna Moth

As a child, I had as much curiosity about nature as a boatload of explorers. 'Why?' was my favourite question. I really wanted to know more about the seasons, the stars, the birds, the storms, the trees, the vanished sabre-toothed tigers, the fireflies, the stones dropped by retreating glaciers, the flowers, the frogs, the sunsets, the quartz crystals, the butterflies and the creatures that only emerged at night.

Which is why, I'm sure, my parents gave me a torch for my ninth birthday. One night in May, I stepped out our kitchen door, trusty torch in hand, and walked over to our apple trees. Switching on the light, I scanned the darkened trunks of the trees, the scraggly grass and the muddy patch I knew well from a recent afternoon spent building a small river and an earthen bridge. Even now, the bridge arched over the waterway like a muddy rainbow.

On this particular night, the moon hadn't yet risen. It was darker than I'd expected. And also quieter. The wind stirred slightly, rustling some leaves. From somewhere nearby on the hillside, an owl hooted. Looking up, I saw the evening's first stars.

Then, aiming the torch at the ground, I looked more closely at the mud at my feet. Something strange caught my eye. It was a handprint in the mud – but wait, how could it be so tiny? The imprint showed long, thin fingers that gripped the ground. A raccoon, I realised. And I felt quite pleased, knowing the evening's explorations had already been successful.

I turned away, sweeping my torch across an apple tree. Suddenly, I jumped in surprise. There, perched on the gnarled trunk, was the biggest butterfly or moth I had ever seen.

A luna moth.

Though I didn't yet know its name, I certainly felt its ethereal presence. Like a sliver of moonlight that had fallen from the sky, this moth seemed to glow mysteriously. I couldn't even begin to describe its otherworldly, green-tinted lustre. Nor could I explain why this discovery felt so deeply strange and deeply magical.

All I knew was that sheer luck had brought me up close to a creature so startling, so elegant and so beautiful, I'd never forget it. Even now, all these years later, that memory is as bright and clear as a rising moon.

CHAPTER 5

Invisible Neighbours

One touch of nature makes the whole world kin.

WILLIAM SHAKESPEARE, *TROILUS AND CRESSIDA*

OCYPODIDAE

Ghost Crab

Scurrying across the beaches of Japan, Hawaiʻi, and other parts of the world, ghost crabs move so fast they seem like a spray of sand, a barely glimpsed blur. They're also nocturnal, so the blur often vanishes into the shadows of twilight or the darkness of a moonless night. Ghosts of the shores.

Appropriately, the scientific name for ghost crabs is *Ocypode*, Greek for 'swift footed'. As with other crabs, they have ten legs, including two bearing claws, and their anatomy allows them to dart sideways but not forwards or backwards. Yet that doesn't slow them down. Like their cousins, the Sally Lightfoot crabs of America's Pacific coast, they can skitter away with lightning speed, disappearing under a rock or into a tide pool. But unlike the flamboyantly coloured Sallys (which were named after an equally flamboyant dancer of the early twentieth century), ghost crabs' pale sandy colour makes them almost invisible.

Heikegani, sometimes called samurai crabs, are found only in Japan. According to Japanese tradition, there is a reason why the shells of these ghost crabs look almost like the faces of people. Legends say it's because the crabs bear the souls of the brave Heike warriors who died in a great war over the imperial throne, the Battle of Dannoura, almost a thousand years ago.

Far across the Pacific Ocean, sand-coloured crabs are also found on the beaches of the Galápagos Islands of Ecuador. These crabs dart so swiftly that if you happen to blink, you'll miss them. They are known by the Spanish name *cangrejos fantasma*. Translation? 'Ghost crabs'.

On the islands of Hawaiʻi, ghost crabs skitter throughout the night, their presence as constant as the waves lapping against the beaches. Their ancient Hawaiʻian name, *ōhiki*, means

c. 1740 | Mark Catesby | *Ocypodidae*

'to probe' because of their habit of digging in the sand for food. Or are they, perhaps, digging for something we cannot see, something as elusive as the ghosts evoked in their name?

The word 'ghost' itself has an intriguing etymology. Most likely, it originated with the Proto-Indo-European word *gheis*, an expression of fear, which was also the source of words in ancient tongues that meant 'frightening' or 'upsetting'. For example, in Avestan (the Iranian that was used in Zoroastrian liturgy), the word referred to something terribly scary. Eventually, *gheis* evolved into *goesten*, the Old English term meaning – you guessed it – 'to scare like a bloodcurdling ghost'. From the same root came the German word *geist*, which carries the same frightful meaning. Like the crabs that bear the word 'ghost' in their name, these words inhabit the nocturnal shores of our minds, barely visible but always lurking in the shadows.

MONODON MONOCEROS
Unicorn of the Sea

So rare they're almost never seen, narwhals swim through the icy waters of the Arctic. Because of their elegant tusks, which can grow into a lance up to 3 metres (10 feet) long, they've been dubbed 'unicorns of the sea'.

Actually, they're cetaceans, kin to other whales, porpoises and dolphins. Like their cousins the beluga whales, orca whales and minke whales, narwhals normally live for fifty to sixty years, although some have been known to live up to twice that long. They rarely migrate, preferring to stay in the Arctic waters of Norway, Greenland and Canada. Their truly distinctive feature is that impressive spiralling tusk, which is, in fact, a supersensitive tooth. Appropriately, the scientific name of these mammals focuses on that feature, calling them *Monodon monoceros* – Latin for 'one tooth, one horn'.

1843 | Georges Cuvier | *Monodon monoceros*

Indigenous peoples of the Arctic region have several names for these creatures – including the Inuktitut term *qilalugaq qernertaq*, which translates roughly to 'the seal is swimming'. Other regional names are *tuugaalik* and *qilalugaq*. One Inuit myth vividly describes the origins of the narwhal. According to the myth, the first narwhal was a woman who twisted her hair into the shape of a long, pointed tusk. Then she was tied securely to a white whale that swam away and dragged her under the surface of the sea, where she drowned – only to return magically as a narwhal.

For ancient Viking sailors, the most striking quality of narwhals wasn't the tusk but rather the mottled grey and white skin, which they thought was similar to the skin of a drowned sailor. Because most of the narwhals seen by the Vikings were that colour, they named these animals *nar hval*, combining the Old Norse words for 'corpse' and 'whale'. (In fact, only young adults are that mottled grey colour. While narwhals start out life as bluish grey, they turn lighter over time, ultimately becoming almost completely white.)

A thousand years ago, when Vikings first brought the tusks of narwhals into European markets, the elegant beauty of those tusks sparked a great deal of attention. People started to wonder what wondrous creatures could have grown them – and, indeed, whether those creatures could possess their own special magic. That's when things got really interesting.

At that time, popular legends told of a fantastical one-horned beast from India that combined the features of many different animals. Those legends were quite famous and had been around for a long time, having begun in South Asia and China at least three thousand years before the time of Christ. (Most likely, the legends originated from someone who had, long ago, sighted a rhinoceros or a wild ox.) The Romans eventually dubbed that legendary beast *unicornus*. With the beautiful narwhal tusks suddenly appearing in Europe, it didn't take long for bards and traders to amend the old legends and paint the modern image of a unicorn. Soon, that mythical being was widely celebrated as an elegant, graceful steed with a perfectly virtuous spirit – and a single, gleaming horn.

All this is proof that truth really is stranger than fiction. In the wondrously unpredictable ways that language and nature can twine together over time, the tusk of a cetacean from the Arctic Ocean somehow merged with the story of a bizarre beast inspired by a rhinoceros from India – resulting in the enduring image of one of humanity's most cherished mythical creatures. The magical powers attributed to unicorns are no more surprising than this true story of how they came to be described as we know them today.

How fitting that we have given narwhals, those Arctic creatures whose tusks have inspired so many magical stories and works of art, a new and beautiful name. For they surely deserve to be called 'unicorns of the sea'.

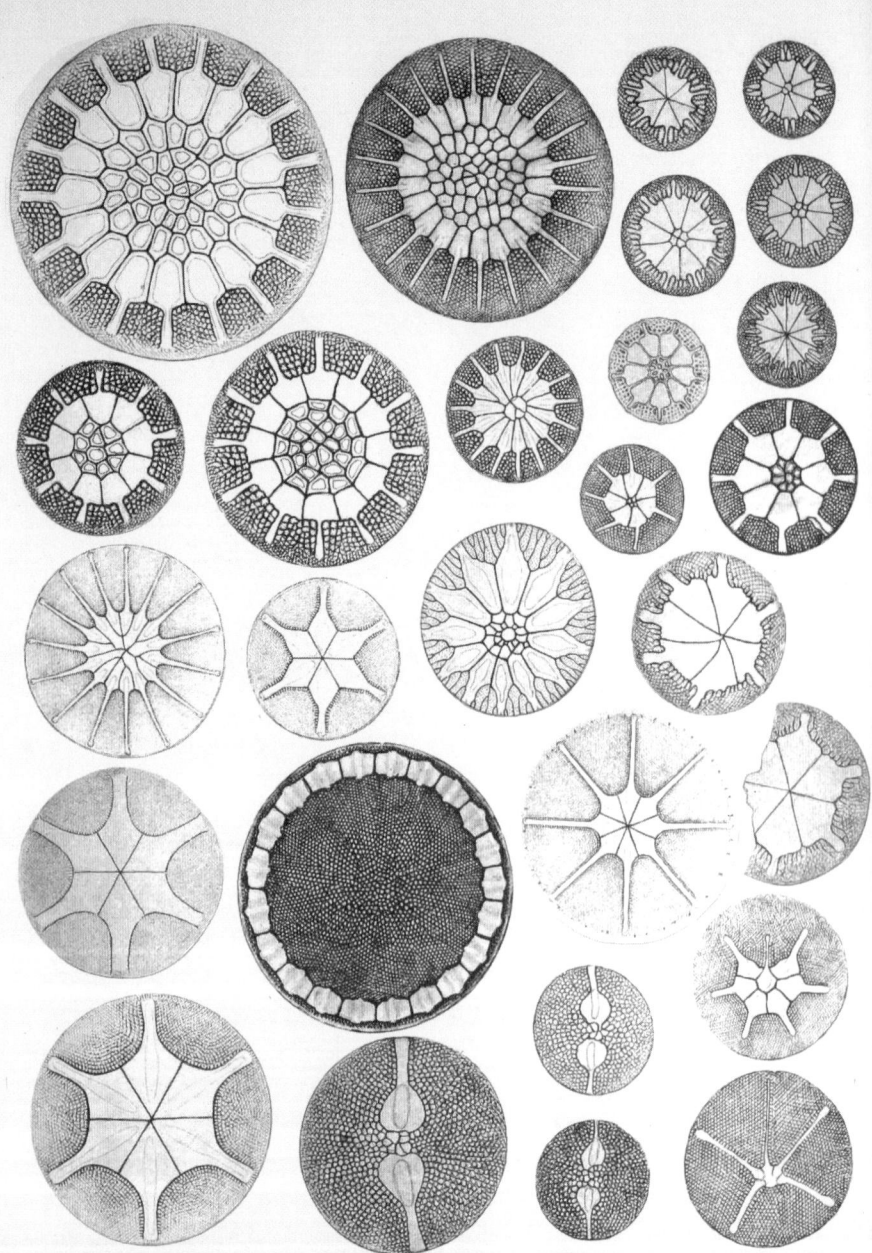

BACILLARIOPHYCEAE
Diatom

Among the smallest life forms on the planet, diatoms are very beautiful – and crucial to sustaining life for all of us. They are so tiny that even a big one is only as wide as one of the hairs atop your head. Yet they are a significant presence in our world, for countless numbers of these microscopic creatures float in all of Earth's oceans.

Diatoms, a kind of algae, build little shells around themselves. Those glassy shells, made from silicon and water, glisten and sparkle with opalescent lustre. Essentially, the shells are extremely small, bejewelled vessels encasing the diatoms. So these creatures are, truly, miniature voyagers that sail the seas in iridescent glass boats. Their importance to life is enormous. Because there are so many of them – more than 200,000 different species – they hold more than one-third of the organic carbon in the ocean and produce nearly one fifth of all the oxygen in our atmosphere through their photosynthesis. They are an essential part of the ocean ecosystem, providing food and crucial nutrients for all sorts of marine life – including fish that are an important food source for humans.

Yet these creatures are at risk. Like every other form of life inhabiting the sea, they are endangered by the rising temperatures caused by human activities, especially the emissions of carbon dioxide from fossil fuels. Those rising temperatures drive increased ocean acidification, which will make less silica available. That, in turn, will make the oceans less hospitable environments for diatoms to live in sustainably.

Despite their significance to the planet, and their ubiquity in the oceans, diatoms are anatomically quite simple. In fact, it's difficult to imagine a more elemental form of life. On the individual level, a diatom is just a single-cell creature that is divided into two parts.

That split into halves is what inspired their name, from the Latin word *diatoma*, meaning 'cut in half'.

Yet that name doesn't come anywhere close to conveying the wonder and beauty of these tiny creatures. It would be like naming an elephant for nothing more than its tusks or its big round footprints. To my mind, diatoms deserve something much better, a name that's evocative of their unique beauty. Such as? Personally, I would choose a name that celebrates the diatoms' exquisite, prismatic shells. Something like . . . *nautis lucidis scaphis*, Latin for 'sailors on luminous boats'.

DOLICHOUSNEA LONGISSIMA

Methuselah's Beard Lichen

Because lichens are known for longevity, it's fitting that this one was named after Methuselah, the undisputed grand elder of the Bible's Old Testament and the grandfather of Noah. Methuselah is described as having clocked 969 years. At such an advanced age, he could have grown a most impressive beard – much like this long, draping lichen found in the boreal forests of Europe and North America.

Its scientific name, *Usnea longissima*, combines terms from two different languages. The word *usnea* (which likely came from the Arabic word *ushnah*, 'moss' or 'lichen') is paired with *longissima*, Latin for 'the longest'.

Indigenous peoples in North America have many names and medicinal uses for this lichen. To the Cree, it's *mithapakwan*; to the Northern Chipewyan people, it's *k'i tsaju*; and to the Blackfoot, it's *e-simatch-sis*. Traditionally, tribes have relied on the soft, absorbent substance for stanching blood flow from wounds, fighting inflammation, and other healing practices.

Other people over time have also turned to this lichen for healing purposes. It's possible that the most famous physician of ancient Greece, Hippocrates, used it to counter urinary troubles. In South African folk medicine, it's used to ease inflammation in people's mouths. Additionally, people are currently studying the lichen's antifungal properties that could potentially be useful in treating conditions such as athlete's foot and yeast overgrowth.

To the Dena'ina people, who are indigenous to the region of Southcentral Alaska and whose Athabaskan language carries deep connections to those lands, this lichen is called *ch'vala andazi*. That translates as the evocative phrase 'spruce hair'. No name could better describe the lichen, sprouting from trunks and branches throughout the forests. Meanwhile, members of the Dakota tribe, who have long lived in the upper Midwest of the United States, have their own poetic name for this lichen. They call it *chan wiziye*, which means 'spirit of the north wind'.

Lichens, as a group, have many other names, some of them rather entertaining. There are varieties called 'hammered shield lichen', 'map lichen' and 'strings of sausage lichen'. As well as 'peppermint drop', 'wart', 'tube', 'witch's hair', 'ruffle', 'bloodstain', 'egg yolk', 'crab's eye', 'dimple', 'fish scale', 'black curly', 'honeycombed' and 'blistered navel'. There is even a lichen labelled 'rock pimples'. Yet as descriptive as those names are, none of them carry the same weight as 'Methuselah's beard'.

But the weight of that lichen's impact on human experience could, alas, be diminishing. While Methuselah's beard can still be found in many places, it has been declining overall and is now considered endangered. That's because one of its most important qualities is completely invisible: this lichen is highly sensitive to air pollution, which can seriously harm its metabolism.

In this way, wise old Methuselah is giving us a clear warning – reminding us that the health and longevity of this particular life form is clearly linked to our own. If we do the right things to combat pollution in our world, we can improve life for all creatures, even as we increase our own chances of living to a ripe old age.

PANTHERA UNCIA

Snow Leopard

'Mountain ghost'. That's the meaning of *schenn*, the name given by the Balti people of India and Pakistan, whose ancestors came long ago from Tibet, to the marvellous creatures we call snow leopards.

Roaming the ridges and snowfields of the High Himalayas and the Karakoram range, these big cats couldn't be more magnificent – or more elusive. For they move like the wind through these mountains. Seeing one, or even just the track of one, feels like a blessing.

The snow leopard holds a place of special significance in the traditions of Tibetan Buddhism. Among the songs of the poet Milarepa, a siddha who lived in the region more than a thousand years ago, 'Song of the Snow Ranges' is among the most cherished. That song tells of Milarepa's experience of being snowbound for several months and how that great adversity led him to deeper spirituality. At one point, his disciples were searching for him and saw a snow leopard in the distance. Later, he explained that he himself had become the snow leopard. Many people view this story as an inspiring parable about living in true harmony with nature and our fellow creatures.

The word 'leopard' has bounded across much linguistic terrain over time. The Ancient Greek word *leon*, meaning 'lion', probably merged with *pardos*, another term used for big cats, especially panthers. That word itself is likely connected to *prdakuh*, a Sanskrit word that could apply to 'leopard' or 'tiger'. Ultimately, the term evolved to the Latin word *leopardus* and then to the Old French *lebard*, the modern French *léopard* and the English *leopard*.

In the enormously rugged terrain where snow leopards live, prey is sparse and difficult to find, so individuals require lots of territory to survive. It's estimated that one adult male's normal range covers 130 square kilometres (80 square miles). That means, for example, the entire country of Singapore could only support three of these big cats; the whole Hawai'ian island of Maui could only hold nine of them.

As the region's top predators, snow leopards are sometimes sighted in India, Pakistan, China, Bhutan and Nepal. But they are increasingly vulnerable. Beyond the normal dangers of avalanches and rockfalls, they now face greater harm from humans. Alas, in recent times, the population of snow leopards has declined dramatically.

1593 | Anselmus de Boodt | *Panthera uncia*

Yet there's still reason for hope. Many people are working hard to protect the habitats of these creatures, which epitomise grace in motion. And there are great additional benefits to successful conservation. By protecting the snow leopards and their territory, we are also protecting many other special forms of life, including Himalayan griffon vultures, Bharal sheep and Asiatic ibex. On top of that, we are securing precious sources of fresh water, which gathers in the mountains and flows down to lower elevations, sustaining millions of people.

Despite these challenges, snow leopards continue to persist – as do the love and respect they inspire in many Himalayan peoples. To the Wakhi, a nomadic tribe that has long travelled the region with its herds of yaks, snow leopards are the mountains' true guardians. Known by many other names, snow leopards are *zigsa* to Tibetans, *irves* to Mongolians, *shan* to Ladakhis and *barfānī chītā* to speakers of Hindi and Urdu. Their Sanskrit name *himanta* (हिमन्तय) means 'covered with snow'.

As for myself, I simply call these creatures 'magnificent'.

TUBERACEAE

Truffle

With their complex, earthy flavour, truffles are edible fungi that have been prized as delicacies by food lovers since the days of the ancient Babylonians. Found only underground, they develop among the roots of oak, beech and chestnut trees, making them rare and difficult to find. Fortunately, dogs and pigs can be trained to detect their unique scent. As a result, humans can experience their intense aroma and flavour ... as well as their intriguing history.

What is the root (so to speak) of this word? It began with *tuber*, Latin for 'edible root'. By the fourteenth century, it had morphed into the French word *trufle*, and then into the English *truffle*. In the past century, the English term has also come to mean a variety of chocolates that look somewhat like the real thing – but taste very different.

Humanity's fascination with truffles stretches way back in time. First described on clay tablets by Babylonians in Mesopotamia four thousand years ago, truffles were also prized in Ancient Egypt. By the time the Greek botanist Theophrastus wrote about them in *Historia Plantarum*, four centuries before the

1896 | Edmund Michael | *Tuberaceae*

birth of Christ, Greek cooks were already making meals with truffles, calling them *hydnón* (ὕδνον). Later, Plutarch, the Greek philosopher and priest at the Temple of Apollo, proposed that truffles were produced by a magical combination of water, heat and lightning. The Roman poet Juvenal went further, proposing that truffles originated from a lightning bolt thrown by none other than Jupiter, the king of the gods. In that spirit, the Roman emperor Nero was said to have called truffles 'the food of the gods'.

For thousands of years, Aboriginal Australians of the Warlpiri, Gugadja and Pintupi communities have used truffles (which they call *bulundari*) as bushfood and medicinal aids. In Southern Africa, the San/Khoisan people of the Kalahari Desert call truffles *kuutse* or *n'xaba* – and value them so much that their mythology considers them 'the eggs of the lightning bird'. In Arab regions, truffles have long been cherished, even though they're difficult to find in the wild. That scarcity is indicated by the Arabic name *kam'ah* (كَمأة), which means 'hidden thing'.

Myths about truffles – and their magical properties – continued to grow, spreading through the cultural landscape like, well, fungi. In medieval times, people expanded on the belief that truffles developed only when lightning struck particular kinds of trees, convinced that only such heavenly powers could produce them. Others championed truffles as potent aphrodisiacs, a quality that is still touted by some people today. Still others strongly disagreed, maintaining that truffles were spawned by sinister, otherworldly beings and should be avoided at all costs. Those folk even called truffles 'devil's dung'.

Folklore added to the mystique, with tales of truffles carrying various additional powers like enhanced fertility. In one medieval tale, a childless couple was terribly despondent, longing to have a family of their own. They prayed fervently to have at least one child, and they tried numerous potions and practices. But nothing helped. Finally, out of desperation, they tried eating truffles. Then, to their astonishment, they had over a dozen children.

Today, the worldwide market for truffles is estimated to be more than 7.5 million pounds (1 billion US dollars) annually. With increasing demand for truffles in gourmet cuisine (especially the much-sought-after white truffles from the Piedmont region of Italy), and with more sustainable agricultural practices, that market is likely to grow. On top of that, people are increasingly using truffles to enhance oils, sauces and beverages. There are also truffle-infused creams that claim to reduce wrinkles and promote healthy skin.

Though some people throughout history have viewed truffles with scepticism, or even as a dangerous source of evil, their appeal has clearly triumphed. They are enormously popular, enjoyed by diners around the world (myself included). For many of us, truffles are a lovely addition to certain meals – cherished for their alluring flavour, their enchanting history and their enduring mystique.

UNCLASSIFIED
Yeti

High in the wilds of the Himalayas lives the yeti, an enormous creature that's part man, part bear and part ape. So believe many Tibetans, at any rate. Though there's never been a reliably confirmed sighting, many Tibetans are certain that yetis exist in the region's high-altitude forests and sheer cliffs. They describe the largest ones as standing nearly 5 metres (about 15 feet) tall, with thick fur, powerful arms and huge feet. Big enough, certainly, to make a lasting impression – with their looks as well as their footprints.

The name 'yeti' originated with the Sherpas, ethnic Tibetans living in some of the most remote parts of the region (mainly in Nepal). They call this creature *ye teh*, translated as 'cliff-dwelling bear'. Their other names are equally evocative: *kangmi*, meaning 'snowman'; *mi shonpo*, meaning 'strong man'; and *metoh*, meaning 'man bear'.

Many people have searched long and hard for yetis without success. Yet the amazing tales about them still thrive. Who hasn't heard of the mysterious 'abominable snowman'? That term was coined in 1921 by a journalist named Henry Newman, based in Calcutta (now Kolkata), who interviewed the Sherpa porters on that year's British reconnaissance mission to Mount Everest. When he asked them about the reports of huge human-like footprints atop the pass Laghpa La at the altitude of 6,400 metres (21,000 feet), they insisted the prints came from the *metoh-kangmi* ('man-bear snowman'). Newman mistranslated those words as the 'abominable snowman' – and ignited a whole new level of speculation about the creature also called 'the wild man of the snows'.

Does this mysterious being really exist? Somewhere up in the most remote reaches of the Himalayas, perhaps, lies the answer. Yet the extreme ruggedness of those snowy mountains will not make any answer easy to find. The name 'Himalaya', in fact, comes from the ancient Sanskrit words *hima*, for 'snow', and *alaya*, for 'home' – reminding any explorers that those forbidding mountains are truly 'the home of the snow'.

Yetis might conceivably have relatives on the other side of the world: Sasquatch and Bigfoot – enormous creatures that some folk believe live in the remote mountains of western Canada and the Pacific Northwest of the United States. (Most likely, the name 'Sasquatch' came from the Indigenous American Salish peoples' word *Sasq'ets*, which means 'wild man'.) As with the yeti, the question of their existence will probably never be fully answered.

It's worth remembering, though, that what's most important here isn't the answer – it's the question. The endless search for the yeti is one of countless examples of humanity's eternal yearning for wonders and mysteries beyond our known universe. There is no limit to what we can imagine, seek or dream.

That's why the raging debates about whether the yeti exists in physical form miss the whole point. For two reasons: first, this creature has held a cherished place in Tibetan lore for a very long time. It's clearly alive and well in a cultural sense. Long may that continue. Second, the yeti belongs in our world – and also in this book – for a different reason. I believe it exists, most of all, to make us wonder. To remind us how little we really know about the natural world. To give us a touch of mystery, as well as a touch of humility – a quality often harder to find than a yeti.

An Encounter with a Snow Leopard

Frosted tufts of grass crackled under my boots in the darkness before dawn as I climbed up a ridge in the Ladakh region of India. This alpine tundra, while steep, was far more passable than the icy mountain summits that rose all around. For very good reasons, the ancient Tibetan name for this region, *La dak*, means 'land of high passes'.

My local guide, Tsering, walked just ahead, his figure a dark shadow on the slope. Deeply knowledgeable about the glaciated landscapes of the Karakoram range and the Himalayas, he also knew well the rich Tibetan culture of his people. It is a culture even more colourful than the prayer flags decorating the region's whitewashed monasteries and mountain passes.

A major point on the ancient trade routes between Tibet, India, China and Kashmir, this valley in Ladakh had for centuries drawn people seeking to buy or sell treasures like silk, salt or wool. And now, in modern times, it had begun to draw people like me who were seeking an entirely different sort of treasure. For I had come here hoping to see one of the most magnificent creatures on the planet. A snow leopard.

Fortunately, Tsering had many years of experience tracking them, as well as their favourite prey, Bharal sheep and Asiatic ibex. Yet there could be no guarantee that we would be lucky enough to catch sight of one. In fact, the first thing Tsering had told me was this: we wouldn't find a snow leopard – but a snow leopard might choose to find us.

For years, I'd dreamt of catching at least a glimpse of this great cat, one of nature's most extraordinary creatures. While I knew that it wouldn't be easy, I felt encouraged by Tsering's expertise. He brought to this challenge the skills of an expert tracker and beyond that, he held a profound reverence for the animal we were seeking. To him, the snow leopard was the very guardian of these mountains.

As we approached the top of the ridge, the first rays of light streamed from the rising sun, illuminating swirling clouds and snowy summits.

Suddenly, Tsering froze, crouched and pointed across a glacier-carved ravine. My heart beat like a line of prayer flags snapping in the wind. Then I saw it. For one brief instant – I watched a leopard move gracefully up a craggy face, pause to scan the surroundings, then disappear completely over the other side. The whole sighting lasted maybe two or three seconds. The last thing I saw was a long, curling, silvery tail as it swept through the air, sharp and clear against the golden clouds.

ChAPTER 6

Strange Swimmers and Slitherers

The Earth has many keys,

Where melody is not

Is the unknown peninsula.

Beauty is nature's fact.

EMILY DICKINSON, 'THE EARTH HAS MANY KEYS'

ELECTROPHORUS ELECTRICUS
Electric Eel

Sometimes our fellow creatures are so bizarre, so otherworldly, they should be described just for sheer amazement. Or for shock value. Take electric eels. Gliding silently through the waters of the Amazon and its surrounding rivers, these creatures are well worth avoiding. Called a 'swarm' when they gather as a group, they are a highly effective band of hunters. Despite their common name, they aren't really eels but rather a kind of knifefish. But they most certainly are electric.

Believe it or not, each one of these creatures has the ability to generate an electric charge of more than 800 volts. That's more than enough to stun a prey fish. Or, indeed, to completely paralyse a human. What's more, an electric eel can regulate the precise amount of voltage produced with every burst of power, so it can use lower bursts to detect potential prey that might be cruising somewhere in the murky water. Through those bursts, it can discern movement that wouldn't otherwise be noticed. It can even communicate with fellow eels about its readiness for breeding. Imagine the message embedded in one of those mating zaps: come here, shall we make some sparks together?

Recently, some Japanese researchers from Nagoya University made a discovery that was, shall we say, electrifying. After extensive study, they concluded that a jolt from one of these eels is actually strong enough to modify the genetic material of fish larvae in the area, much the same way that a bolt of lightning has been known to alter the genetic makeup of soil bacteria.

In Venezuela, Indigenous peoples have wonderfully apt names for these creatures. In the language of Tupi, spoken in parts of Brazil, they are called *puraké,* meaning 'the ones that numb'. Others call the eels *arimna,* which translates to 'things that

c. 1843 | James Hope Stewart | *Gymnotus electricus*

deprive you of motion'. Similarly, the first European observers called these creatures 'numb eels'.

The earliest description of electric eels by a European was made way back in 1583 by a Jesuit priest from Portugal, Fernão Cardim. So it's not surprising that the word 'eel' itself has been swimming for centuries in the rivers of human language. The origins of the word can be traced back to the Latin word *anguis,* for 'snake'. Influence also came from Old German, which used the term *ælaz*. Eventually, the word *æl* appeared in Old English, and that ultimately became 'eel'.

Scientists call these eels *Electrophorus electricus*, highlighting the importance of their most astonishing feature, their ability to produce electricity. In fact, studying the specialised anatomy of electric eels over two hundred years ago helped the Italian inventor Alessandro Volta to design the first manufactured battery. That influential invention is used widely today to power everything from phones to cars to buildings.

LITORIA PINOCCHIO

Pinocchio Frog

This rare Indonesian tree frog, recently discovered by scientists in the rainforest of New Guinea, exemplifies the immense biodiversity of that island famous for its unique, beautiful and spectacular creatures. It's only one of hundreds of varieties of amphibians that live there in remote, secluded habitats – including one with the remarkable name 'gargoyle-faced gecko'.

The discovery of this frog was made by Paul Oliver, an Australian herpetologist at the Queensland Museum in Brisbane, which is dedicated to natural history and cultural heritage. Upon seeing its very long, pointed nose, he decided to name it after – who else? – Pinocchio, the beloved character from the nineteenth-century novel by Italian writer Carlo Collodi. As most people are aware, Pinocchio's nose would unfailingly grow longer every time he told a lie. It's fair to say that his nose is the most famous schnozzle in all of literature – along with that of Cyrano de Bergerac, the character dramatised by the French writer Edmond Rostand. (For those who can sniff out an interesting word origin . . . the word 'schnozzle' originally came from the Yiddish word *shnoits*, meaning 'snout'.)

What was the origin of the name Pinocchio? Nobody is certain – and if anyone tells you otherwise, watch their nose very carefully, for it's sure to grow longer. Most likely, the name resulted from combining two Italian words – *pino*, meaning 'pine tree', and *occhio*, meaning 'eye'.

In Tok Pisin, the Creole language used widely in Papua New Guinea, the name for 'frog' is beautifully onomatopoeic. To speakers of Tok Pisin, these creatures are *prok* or *rokrok*. Just saying those names out loud conjures up the sound of frogs calling at night in the rainforest.

In a similar vein, the Latin word for 'frog', *rana*, sounds very much like one of these creatures making its commonly heard vocalisation. So does the Slovenian word, *zhaba*. As well as the Swahili word, *chura*. And the Laotian word, *gop*. These are just a few of the many lovely examples of words in every language that are inspired by nature's voices.

Scientists are still mystified about why this particular frog, known to them as *Litoria pinocchio*, has such a truly distinctive nose. Perhaps it evolved to attract mates, to vocalise special calls, or identify others of its species. Any of those could be possible. Or, who knows? Maybe the nose is really there to reveal when a frog has been telling lies?

AMBLYRHYNCHUS CRISTATUS
Marine Iguana

Among the world's strangest animals, marine iguanas live in only one place, the Galápagos Islands of Ecuador. The name of those famous islands originated with a Spaniard, Bishop Tomás de Berlanga, who landed there almost five hundred years ago. (Mind you, he didn't arrive there intentionally – he had actually planned to sail to Peru.) Stuck there until someone answered his prayers and came to rescue him, he busied himself checking out the surroundings. He found them rocky and desolate, uninhabited except for some intriguing creatures. After he was, at last, rescued, he did his best to describe those creatures in a letter to his ruler, Emperor Charles V of Spain. That letter was circulated widely among European scholars.

Most of all, Berlanga liked the tortoises. Noting the shape of their shells, he called them *galápagos* because they reminded him of a kind of saddle by that name. Not long after that, a Flemish mapmaker, Abraham Ortelius, who had seen a copy of the letter to the Spanish crown, labelled the whole archipelago *Insulae de Los Galápagos* (a short way of saying 'The Islands Where You Can Find Turtles Whose Shells Look Somewhat Like Saddles'). The name Galápagos stuck.

And so, in yet another example of the surprising randomness of how names may evolve, these islands got their name not from any prominent natural feature, notable landmark or legend. No. They got their name from the particular shape of a kind of tortoise shell that happened to remind someone from another continent, centuries ago, of a saddle.

1876 | Franz Steindachner | *Amblyrhynchus cristatus*

To survive on those islands, marine iguanas have developed a highly specialised skill. Unlike any other kind of lizard, they have the ability to gather algae right from the ocean. While many of them forage continuously in the intertidal waters, the biggest males hunt for algae underwater, sometimes staying submerged for an hour.

But to my mind, the most impressive skill of these reptiles is something else – their ability to ingest seawater. That's right – they can drink the very brine of the sea. Thanks to special glands in their nostrils, marine iguanas can swallow saltwater, filter the salt out of their bloodstream and then expel the unwanted waste by sneezes. How many sailors and castaways, desperate for drinkable water, would have loved to perform such a feat?

In Spanish, these reptiles are called *iguana marina*, identical in meaning to the English name. What is the source of the word 'iguana'? It came originally from the Arawak language of the Caribbean region, where these lizards were originally known as *iwana*. The scientific name for marine iguanas is *Amblyrhynchus cristatus*, chosen by an English zoologist, Thomas Bell. *Cristatus*, the Latin word for 'crested', is an appropriate way to describe the spiky crest that runs up the backs of these reptiles, which makes them look a lot like miniature dinosaurs.

As tough and resilient as these animals are, they remain vulnerable to El Niño climatic events. Those events and their consequences can reduce marine iguanas' food supply significantly. For now, though, these longtime residents of the Galápagos Islands continue to ride the waves of time and fate.

STRANGE SWIMMERS AND SLITHERERS

CRYPTOBRANCHUS ALLEGANIENSIS
Hellbender

What animal in America's Appalachian Mountains has different numbers of toes on its front and back legs, can breathe through its skin and is so ugly that it's been considered a monster from the realms of eternal damnation? Allow me to introduce you to the hellbender. Why such a loaded name? Before we turn to that intriguing story, let's take a closer look at the creature that must live with the name.

To be sure, these salamanders aren't the prettiest-looking creatures. Slimy and blotchy, with heads so flat they seem to have been crushed, along with heavy layers of rippled skin, they are not what you would call beautiful. Yet they are still quite impressive. For starters, they are North America's biggest amphibian. Hellbenders can grow as long as 60 centimetres (2 feet) and weigh up to 2.5 kilogrammes (5½ pounds).

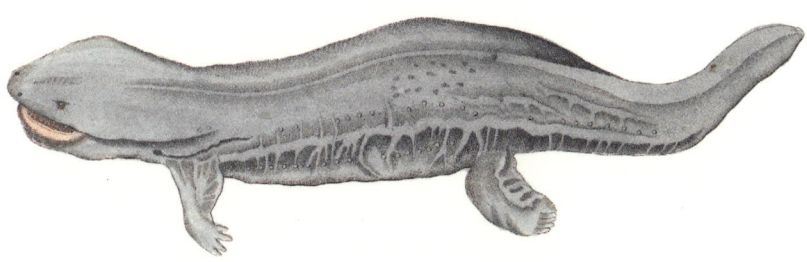

c. 1800 | Unknown/Iconographia Zoologica | *Cryptobranchus alleganiensis*

In addition, hellbenders are well adapted to life in fast-moving, unpolluted streams. They have lungs but don't really need them. Spending their lives underwater, in well-oxygenated currents, they can breathe entirely through the pores of their layered skin. That ability to breathe underwater gave rise to the first part of their scientific name, *Cryptobranchus*, which means 'secret gills'. That term combines the Greek words *krytos* ('secret') and *branchos* ('gills'). The rest of their scientific name, *alleganiensis*, is the Latin term indicating they live in the Allegheny region of the Appalachians.

To the Indigenous Cherokee people, who often found them in streams and ponds, these salamanders were simply *tsu-wa*, meaning 'water dogs'. But in more recent times, people who had arrived from Europe gave them more pejorative names, such as 'mud devils', 'Allegheny alligators' or 'devil dogs'. Others called them 'snot otters' (because of the animals' ability to secrete protective mucus).

Why such negative names? Sometime after the new settlers encountered hellbenders, rumours started to spread that these harmless creatures were dangerous to the fish in the rivers. People claimed, wrongly, that the salamanders would eat trout as well as trout eggs. Other rumours asserted they were venomous. All this led to killing sprees, sometimes rewarded with bounties. Even as their population declined, hellbenders also suffered from river pollution and habitat destruction during the Industrial Revolution. By the middle of the twentieth century, they were on the verge of dying out completely. Only the Clean Water Act of 1972, which encouraged the restoration of rivers and streams, saved them from extinction. Even now, their survival is precarious.

So, all those pejorative names probably stemmed from the false notion that these animals preyed on trout. Together with their unappealing looks, that notion doomed many of them. Yet why would they also be associated with hell? Most likely that stemmed from the longstanding myth that salamanders actually thrive in flames. Dating back to Aristotle, philosophers and storytellers have claimed that salamanders are born from fire and can even control flames at will.

Some writers, such as the seventeenth-century minister John Flavel, took that idea further. In his sermons (which spewed plenty of fire and brimstone), Flavel connected salamanders to images of sin and eternal damnation. The connection with hell deepened over time. Eventually, across the Atlantic Ocean, an unsuspecting salamander took on the name 'hellbender'. And with that name, sadly, came a rather hellish existence.

It's safe to say that hellbenders don't mind being called ugly. Nor do they mind being called invaders from the underworld. But they clearly do mind any pollution of the streams where they live, which is why they remain endangered today. They can still be saved, but that will require us to make more thoughtful choices, to do a better job of protecting the habitats around us – including the waterways of these peaceful creatures.

If humans could rise to that level of awareness, that would, indeed, be heavenly.

CORALLUS CANINUS
Emerald Tree Boa

As vibrant green as the Amazon rainforest where it lives, the emerald tree boa is one of the world's most beautiful snakes. Like all boa constrictors, it's not venomous – but if you happen to be a bird or small mammal within reach, it will detect your body heat, wrap its powerful body around you and quickly squeeze you to death.

That's not all the remarkable qualities of these snakes. A female tree boa gives birth to live young that have hatched from eggs inside herself (an unusual ability that makes her 'ovoviviparous', one of the most fun scientific terms ever to say out loud). The biggest of these boa constrictors grow as long as 2.7 metres (9 feet) and blend perfectly into the tropical foliage.

The name boa comes from the Latin *boa*, meaning 'large serpent'. Although no one knows the exact origins of the Latin term, it might have come from the Albanian word *bālwā*, which referred to some kinds of snakes. The first recorded use of the term boa was almost two thousand years ago in Pliny the Elder's *Naturalis Historia*. (Alas, his final revisions of that masterwork were interrupted by the deadly eruption of Mount Vesuvius... so his time for writing was, you might say, severely constricted.)

1876 | Georges Cuvier | *Corallus caninus*

1913 | J Green | *Dendrobates*

DENDROBATIDAE
Poison Dart Frog

Among the most vividly coloured frogs of South America are some that truly deserve to be called poisonous. And the various kinds of poison dart frogs, when found in the wild, are seriously poisonous. Take, for example, the 'golden poison dart frog'. Although it's quite small, only 2.5 to 5 centimetres (1 to 2 inches) long, the toxin from just one of these frogs is strong enough to kill more than a dozen people – or thousands of smaller animals. Predators usually keep their distance, aware that merely touching one of these frogs can cause severe nausea or sometimes even paralysis. Such extreme toxicity makes this little frog the most poisonous creature on Earth, which is why scientists have named its species *terribilis*.

The Indigenous Emberá Chocó people, who live in the rainforest of Colombia on the Pacific side of the Andes, call these frogs *kokoi*. They have long used the frogs' toxin to make blow darts for hunting. Having learnt how to handle the creatures carefully, they can make up to fifty deadly darts from just one frog.

One intriguingly named variety is called 'dyeing' – as distinguished from 'dying'. They were named not for their toxicity but for their bright red, yellow or blue colours (which signal their toxicity to potential predators). In addition to their vivid colours, dyeing poison dart frogs also carry an element of mystery. According to a legend that has never been confirmed, some Indigenous peoples in the Amazon rainforest have used these frogs to change the colours of parrots' feathers from green to red. Though it remains unproven, the legend gave rise to the frogs' species name, *tinctorius*, which is the Latin for 'used for dyeing'.

Other kinds of poison dart frogs also have vividly descriptive names. There's one called 'strawberry', another called 'sky blue' and another called 'bumblebee'. Poison dart frogs in the scientific genus *Ranitomeya* are commonly called 'Brazilian' or 'spotted'. Yet another kind bears a frightening name: 'phantasmal'. (That's one I definitely don't want to meet while hiking somewhere deep in the rainforest.) Still another variety of these frogs is called *oophaga*. That's the Greek term for 'egg eater'. Why did this variety get such a name? Because that's exactly what the tadpoles eat, dining on the unfertilised eggs laid by their own mother.

Anura is the scientific name for all frogs. While the meaning in Latin is 'without a tail', the same word in Sanskrit means 'beautiful' or 'delightful'. Both meanings are true for most frogs – and the gorgeous colours of poison dart frogs can certainly be called 'beautiful'. But if you happen to be unlucky enough to get poisoned by one in the rainforest, you would probably not use that word to describe the experience.

Despite their potency, both in their powerful toxins and in their powerful hold on our imaginations, poison dart frogs are in trouble. Today, they are threatened by the loss of their natural habitat through worsening deforestation. They are also threatened by the international market for rare pets, which creates an incentive for people to steal them from their natural environment and take them elsewhere. Poison, alas, can take many forms in our world.

AMBYSTOMA MEXICANUM

Axolotl

Unique in the natural world, this Mexican salamander has a truly spectacular ability to repair itself and regenerate its own body. That might sound like magic – but it's scientifically verifiable. The axolotl can heal quickly from injuries, restore damaged tissues and easily take transplanted organs. And that's not all. So capable is this little creature, it can completely regrow a lost limb or detached tail. It can even accomplish that same feat with highly complex parts of its brain, eyes and heart.

What's more, the axolotl is neotenic, meaning it has the ability to keep its juvenile form. It can even reproduce as a juvenile.

1867 | Leopold Joseph Fitzinger | *Ambystoma mexicanum*

That's different from other amphibians such as frogs and toads, which take new forms as they grow into adulthood. The term 'neotenic' combines two Greek words, *neos* (νέος), meaning 'young', and *teínein* (τείνειν), meaning 'to extend longer'. So, in addition to its extraordinary ability to regenerate itself . . . this creature, much like Peter Pan, never grows up. Which leads to a naming question: What is the correct term for a baby axolotl? Most scientists call them 'larvae', and many people call them 'pups'. But if you ask me . . . I would say the best name for a baby axolotl is an 'axolittle'.

While axolotls are amazingly capable creatures, one thing they can't do is to find new habitats when their freshwater ones become polluted or destroyed by human development. Sadly, too much of that has occurred in recent decades. So today, while many axolotls exist in pet shops, home aquariums and medical research labs (as well as the video game *Minecraft*), they are seriously endangered in the wild.

The name 'axolotl' has roots in the ancient language Nahuatl. Once the main language of the Aztec empire, it is still spoken by around 2 million people in Mexico. Combining two Nahuatl words, *atl* for 'water' and *xolotl* for 'monster', these little 'water monsters' were named in honour of Xolotl, a powerful god in Aztec mythology. As the god of monstrous beasts, as well as fire and death, Xolotl could transform himself into many beings, including a salamander. In one myth, he even transformed into a stalk of maize. Aztec art often shows him as a man with the head of a dog. The tales of this god's adventures are many. Yet as amazing as they are, they're no more amazing than the actual reality of the axolotl, the wondrous living creature that was named in his honour.

BRACHYCEPHALUS EPHIPPIUM
Pumpkin Toadlet

Small as the tip of your finger, the pumpkin toadlet is the world's tiniest vertebrate. This diminutive resident of the Brazilian rainforest is so small it can't even jump well. One of its eggs is barely bigger than a grain of sand. So it's called a 'toadlet', the smallest possible version of a toad.

No bigger than about 2 centimetres (¾ inch) when fully grown, how does this little creature defend itself against predators? As with other rainforest frogs and toads, the answer is neurotoxin. Its skin secretes a dangerous poison that can bring an attacker's whole nervous system to a crashing halt.

The pumpkin toadlet signals that danger by its vivid colour – as bright as a pumpkin, which inspired its name. (And just in case any predator didn't notice its colour in the sun's full spectrum, this frog's bones glow eerily in fluorescent light.) Like a bright orange sign, this very small creature warns of very large danger. In Brazil, the Portuguese name for this creature also refers to its bright-as-sunrise colour. It's called *botão-de-ouro*, which translates as 'gold button'.

Other kinds of toadlets also have entertaining names. Can you imagine, for example, the 'wrinkled toadlet'? Or the 'red-groined toadlet'? Then there's a 'marbled toadlet', a 'fat toadlet', and a 'dusky toadlet'.

My personal favourite name for a toadlet is the 'tiny toadlet'. While at first that seems like calling an insect 'a small gnat' or 'a small aphid', it's appropriate. This little toadlet, found only in the Kimberley region of northern Australia, is small enough that its scientific species name is *micra* (which is Latin for, essentially, 'teensy weensy'). However, it's worth noting that it's still bigger than the true champion of smallness among these creatures, the pumpkin toadlet.

An Encounter with a Marine Iguana

Since childhood, I've felt drawn to the Galápagos Islands of Ecuador. How could I possibly ignore the allure of so many creatures found nowhere else on Earth? I could almost hear their siren calls – or, putting that less poetically but more accurately, their barks, grunts, shrieks, cries and snorts.

And so, for decades, I dreamt of watching giant tortoises strut on the land, tiny Galápagos penguins swim in the frothy waters, enormous sea lions bask along the coast and magnificent frigate birds soar through the skies. But most of all, I longed to see marine iguanas, those monstrously weird lizards that inhabit the shores.

In my forties, my dream finally came true. There I was, sitting on a rough lava rock splashed by ocean waves, watching a big male iguana. Drawing a deep breath of briny air, I focused all my attention on him. Except for his head, which was encrusted with white salt, he was as black as the lava rock on which he sat. His sturdy limbs, ending in partially webbed feet, grasped the rock, as his head's bony scales rose into a point like an armoured headdress. Along his back, a spiney ridge poked upwards, while his hefty tail lay flat against the stone.

Like a miniature dinosaur that had survived into the modern era, he simply sat there, completely in command of his perch. Occasionally, he turned this way or that, gazing at the other, smaller iguanas as they foraged for algae in the shallows. But mainly he remained as still as a jagged piece of driftwood that had long ago washed ashore. He seemed utterly oblivious to the orange Sally Lightfoot crabs skittering past his feet or the wide-winged albatross that sailed overhead.

Suddenly – he sneezed. That loud eruption scared a nearby seagull so badly, it squawked in alarm, flapping its wings excitedly. But the iguana took no notice. That sneeze, I knew, had expelled sea salt from his body, a wonder of the lizard's unique metabolism.

Lifting his head a little higher, he scanned the surroundings. Then, to my surprise, he leapt off the rock and splashed into the shallows. Slowly, he worked his way out to deeper water. I watched him swim away from shore – until, in the blink of an eye, he plunged downwards. The iguana vanished completely. He left only a faint trace of bubbles . . . and a memory I'll never forget.

CHAPTER 7

Magnificent Mammals

The elephant...

Oldest they are and the wisest of beasts

D. H. LAWRENCE, 'THE ELEPHANT IS SLOW TO MATE'

URSUS AMERICANUS KERMODEI
Spirit Bear

Sacred to the First Nations peoples of Canada, spirit bears are completely white. Like a patch of sunlit snow on a darkened mountainside, they cannot be missed when seen amid the ancient spruce and fir trees of British Columbia's Great Bear Rainforest.

These rare bears, found only in those remote forests of western Canada, have inspired the lasting devotion of the Indigenous Kitasoo Xai'xais and Gitga'at peoples. To them, the spirit bear is known as *mooksgm'ol*, which means 'white bear'. Firmly embedded in Indigenous culture and traditions, spirit bears are seen as enduring signs of peace and harmony, and are the source of many legends. In one traditional story, the Creator Raven made these bears with a sacred purpose – to remind people to feel grateful for the many gifts of nature.

The bears are sometimes called 'Kermode bears', because they were originally thought to be a separate species and were given that name by taxonomists in honour of Francis Kermode, who served as director of the Royal British Columbia Museum in Victoria. Later, scientists concluded that the bears aren't a separate species after all but a rare subspecies of North American black bears. In any case, most people (myself included) prefer to call them by the much more evocative name 'spirit bears'.

c. 1600 | Anselmus de Boodt | *Ursus*

While these bears are in the same family as black bears, a recessive gene makes them white. Technically, they aren't considered albinos, because they still have some skin pigmentation under their fur. And there's an unexpected benefit to their unusual colouration: recent studies have shown that spirit bears are notably more successful than other bears at fishing for salmon in the wild rivers. Why? Probably because the fish have difficulty seeing their white fur.

To the Kitasoo Xai'xais and Gitga'at, spirit bears hold great significance, both culturally and spiritually. For a long time, these people closely guarded the secret of the bears' existence, as a way to save them from European hunters. Fortunately, they succeeded. The dedication of these communities to protecting spirit bears – and their longstanding connection to those magnificent creatures – is inspiring for people everywhere.

DUGONG DUGON

Dugong

'Ladies of the sea'. That's one of many nicknames for these gentle marine mammals. Because they graze calmly on seagrass, they're also called 'sea cows'. Their primary name, dugong, came from *dugung*, a word in the Visayan language of the central Philippines. That word itself most likely had roots in some of the ancient tongues of Malaysia and Polynesia.

Grazing on seagrass in bays and mangrove channels of the western Pacific, Australia and eastern Africa, dugongs have been found in places as diverse as Australia, Japan, Taiwan, Vietnam, the Philippines, Kenya, Tanzania and Mozambique. Immense in size, they grow to more than 3 metres (10 feet) long and weigh over 450 kilogrammes (1,000 pounds). Dugongs have tusks as well as the teeth they use to forage aquatic plants.

Like their cousins, the manatees, dugongs might have inspired the very first tales of wondrous mermaids swimming gracefully in the sea. And that's not their only connection to mythology. Dugongs and manatees are together known by scientists as *Sirenia*, a name that was inspired by the sirens of Greek myths. Yet unlike those legendary sirens who tried to lure sailors to their deaths – including Odysseus as well as Jason and the Argonauts – real-world sirenians are peaceful herbivores that simply like to swim in the shallows. While the legendary sirens sang with irresistible voices, dugongs and manatees are content to graze quietly.

Not so long ago, there was one more member of the family of sirenians: the Steller's sea cow (named for eighteenth-century German naturalist Georg Wilhelm Steller). While dugongs are certainly not small, the Steller's sea cow was truly gigantic. An adult could grow to over 9 metres (30 feet) – more than three times the size of a dugong, and bigger than an orca whale.

1880 | Hugh Craig | *Dugong dugon*

Native to the waters of the North Pacific, they were first spotted by European sailors in the middle of the eighteenth century. Soon the word spread that these huge creatures could be hunted with ease, especially because of their gentle dispositions. Sadly, they were rapidly slaughtered for their meat by sailors in the commercial fur trade. Just twenty-seven years after it had been discovered by Europeans, the Steller's sea cow went extinct, gone forever from the waters of our world.

Dugongs and manatees needn't suffer the same terrible fate. We have the power to help them, and we must. Many dedicated conservationists around the world are doing what they can to help, building strong alliances with local fishing communities, forward-thinking governments, businesses, non-profit groups and caring people near and far. Together, they are striving to create safe zones and marine parks for these beautiful creatures.

The simple truth is, humans can be the primary destroyers of life . . . or the ultimate protectors of it. To my mind, humanity's greatness lies not in how robustly we can control other creatures or how dramatically we can transform the landscapes and seascapes around us. Rather, our greatness lies in *our ability to resist doing those very things*. In our ability to view ourselves as companions of our fellow creatures and stewards of our precious ecosystems. In our ability to live on Earth more wisely, more lovingly, more ethically and more graciously.

ELEPHANTIDAE

Elephant

No land animals on Earth are bigger than elephants. Like their extinct relatives, the well-named 'mammoths', they are truly immense. Found in Africa and Asia, they regularly walk great distances over grassy plains and forests – which is why the collective term for them is 'a parade of elephants'. And wherever they go, they leave tracks across many vital and varied landscapes.

Likewise, the names for these majestic creatures have left tracks across many vital and varied languages. The paths on that linguistic terrain are complex and mysterious, touching languages as diverse as Ancient Greek (ἐλέφας, or *elephas*), Old Norse (*úlfaldi*), Hebrew (*eleph*), Old French (*oliphant*) and Latin (*elephantus*), as well as other possible languages, including Phoenician, Egyptian, Germanic, Slavonic and Sanskrit.

My favourite names for elephants come from African languages. Inspired by the enormous size of these creatures, which are big enough to topple and crush trees, the names in Zulu, Tsonga and Tswana all focus on immensity. And they all mean, essentially, 'impossible to stop'. The Zulu name for elephants, *indlovu*, is also related to the term for 'crashing through'. (These are, as you can tell, rather weighty word origins.)

The most revealing – and most disturbing – aspect of European names for elephants is that, for many centuries, the word simply meant 'ivory'. Around 700 BCE, when Homer and Hesiod wrote about *elephas*, they were describing just the commodity of tusks. So the name applied only to that commodity, something people could buy or sell in the marketplace – not to the magnificent animal that actually produced those tusks. It took a long time (at least two thousand years) before people started using the word 'elephant' to describe the entire living creature.

1830 | Robert Huish | *Elephantidae*

Such longstanding habits are hard to break. Even today, alas, hunters call elephants simply 'tuskers'. This reduction of animal to commodity eliminates any consideration of the elephants themselves. It denies their existence as creatures with amazing abilities, as our companions on this planet and as sources of inspiration to people everywhere. What a loss that is, to effectively erase from human awareness a creature that's so impressive and compelling!

Consider this: elephants are so intelligent they can vocalise specific names for their companions, recognise themselves in the mirror and even paint pictures by holding a paintbrush with their trunks. So capable they have more than forty thousand muscles in their fabulously flexible trunks (compared to less than seven hundred muscles in an entire human body). And so sensitive they show real grief whenever they lose family members, visiting the bones of their lost ones and stroking them gently.

It's easy to understand why elephants are cherished symbols of wisdom and intelligence in many cultures around the world. They figure prominently in religions and mythologies, ranging from the Kamba people in Kenya to Hindus in India to Buddhists in Thailand. And they are beloved by people young and old on every continent.

Even so, elephants are now in danger of extinction. The two main causes are the continued slaughter by poachers who crave their tusks, and the ongoing destruction of elephants' natural habitat. Currently, both species of African elephant are critically endangered.

Will we humans do whatever it takes to protect these wondrous, intelligent, beautiful creatures? It's up to us to decide. The consequences of our choices will be, in every sense, enormous.

MAGNIFICENT MAMMALS

ORNITHORHYNCHUS ANATINUS

Platypus

Seriously, what could be more bizarre than a platypus? This unique creature, swimming in the waters of Australia, has the bill of a duck, the feet of an otter, the tail of a beaver and the venom of a scorpion. In addition, unlike almost any other mammal, it lays eggs like a bird.

When eighteenth-century European scientists first studied a preserved sample of a platypus, they were quite confused. One of them, German biologist Johann Friedrich Blumenbach, proposed giving this odd creature the species name *paradoxus* – the Latin word for 'puzzling'. Other people, more sceptical, thought the whole thing was just a hoax. They argued, how could such a bizarre animal even exist? They concluded that the sample must have been stitched together from several different animals.

1811 | Thomas Busby | *Ornithorhynchus anatinus*

Aboriginal peoples, who were the first to encounter the platypus, were themselves struck by its oddities. In one Aboriginal tale, the platypus appeared when a male water rat (who was both charming and persuasive) got together with a female duck (who was both adventurous and free-thinking). They had children who shared the physical qualities of both, with thick fur as well as webbed feet.

The Aboriginal peoples gave this creature many distinctive names. Depending on the Australian region, it's called *mallingong, biladurang, tambreet, oornie, watjarang, dyiimalung* or *boondaburra*. (My personal favourite is that last one, *boondaburra*, which somehow sounds like just the right name for this animal.)

The name platypus is derived from two Greek words, *platys* ('broad or flat') and *pous* ('foot'). The collective noun for describing a group of them is wonderfully alliterative – 'a paddle of platypuses'. The most adorable name associated with this paradoxical creature is the one for its offspring. A baby platypus is called a 'puggle'.

The scientific name, like the animal itself, is unique as well as confusing: *Ornithorhynchus anatinus*, two terms meaning 'bird-like snout' and 'duck-like'. Meanwhile, scientists classify the platypus in the order *Monotremata*, the only kind of mammals that produce their young by laying eggs. It's also the world's oldest order of living mammals.

There we have it – a rare creature whose stories about its name are as weird, puzzling and surprising as the animal itself. Which is very weird, puzzling and surprising, indeed! A platypus, after all, combines many qualities that would seem so contradictory as to be impossible in any other animal. It is a creature that is duck-billed, fur-backed, beaver-tailed and flat-footed – and also, let's not forget, able to lay eggs and wield a poisonous stinger.

By the way, if you're ever talking about these quirky creatures at a cocktail party, the plural of platypus isn't 'platypuses' (despite what some dictionaries may say). So is the right word 'platypi'? Nope. Since the name came originally from Greek, the plural is actually 'platypodes'. (It's pronounced *pla-TIH-puh-deez*, which rhymes with the name of the Greek playwright Euripides.)

Too tricky to remember? Don't worry. It's highly unlikely that anyone will ever correct you if you just decide to call them 'platypuses'.

PAN TROGLODYTES

Chimpanzee

The name of these animals originated with Tshiluba, a Bantu language from Central Africa's Congo region. The Tshiluba term *chimpenze* translates as 'mockman' – a nod to how similar these great apes are to ourselves. Moving into other languages, the term became *chimpanzee*, which first appeared in print in a 1738 edition of *London Magazine*. Scientists later dubbed them *Pan troglodytes*. They included *Pan* as a salute to the Greek god of wild nature, while *troglodytes* arose from the mistaken belief that chimpanzees lived in caves.

What's the collective noun for chimps? In fact, there are several possibilities. Some people say 'a troop', while others prefer 'a group'. Still others say 'a cartload of chimpanzees'. My preference, though, is to use the term I learnt from a primatologist, who called them 'a whoop of chimpanzees'.

These creatures are (with bonobos) our closest relatives in the natural world. And they really do resemble their human cousins. In addition to displaying unique personalities, chimpanzees can communicate vocally, walk upright and build strong social bonds. They are also highly intelligent and curious about the world around them.

Significantly, Jane Goodall found that chimpanzees can make and use tools – a momentous discovery that actually redefined what it means to be human. Before that time, scientists thought only humans could perform such a feat. But she revealed that clever chimps knew how to bend a branch, remove its leaves and then use it to extract termites from their nest.

Chimpanzees range across western and Central Africa. But human population growth now threatens much of their natural environment. If they are going to survive, to remain

1847 | Charles Dessalines d'Orbigny | *Pan troglodytes*

our companions on this planet, they will need our help. To my mind, our essential human quality – what truly makes us human – never really was the ability to make tools. No, it's something else, something even more essential to our nature. It's *our ability to tell stories.* In particular, complex stories that carry abstract concepts. Stories that create metaphors, envision the future, convey deep emotions and hold enduring ideas.

Wouldn't it be wonderful to create a story, right now, that celebrates the bond between humans and chimpanzees? Let's tell a story with our lives that connects these two extraordinary species, beings who have been evolutionary relatives for millions of years. And let's make sure it's a story about living together in harmony for all time.

PHASCOLARCTOS CINEREUS

Koala

While all animals are adorable as babies, no adult animal is more adorable than a koala. So it's entirely understandable that this furry leaf eater has enchanted humans for thousands of years, evidenced by the sweet portraits of koalas in ancient Aboriginal cave paintings.

Along with the kangaroo and the wallaby, the koala is closely identified with Australia. Like the other two, it's a marsupial, carrying its little ones in a pouch for about six months. Those young koalas are commonly called 'joeys'.

The name 'koala' has Indigenous roots. Like the words 'kangaroo' and 'didgeridoo', it came from Australia's Aboriginal peoples. In the Dharug language, long spoken in Australia until the arrival of Europeans, koalas were called *gula*, which means 'no water'. That's because these creatures dine exclusively on the leaves of gum (eucalyptus) trees, which provide most of the water they need. So they rarely climb down from their arboreal perches to drink.

This story about the word *gula*, which has evolved to 'koala', is just one of many examples of the importance of names for the Aboriginal peoples. Due to their deep spiritual and physical connection to the land now called Australia, they gave thoughtful names to all its places, creatures, elements and geographical features. Those names comprise a rich treasury of experiences and traditions. While they differ depending on the language and region, Aboriginal names were always chosen with great care and respect for the land itself.

The name 'Australia' stems from the Latin *auster*, meaning 'south wind' or 'land of the south'. For centuries, Europeans believed that a mysterious southern continent might exist, and

1863 | John Gould | *Phascolarctos cinereus*

they called it *Terra Australis Incognita*, Latin for 'Unknown Southern Land'. When Dutch explorer Abel Tasman sailed through the region in the mid-seventeenth century, he called the continent 'New Holland', but others preferred 'Terra Australis'. Finally, in 1804, the English explorer Matthew Flinders proposed 'Australia'.

Despite the common name 'koala bear' and its strong resemblance to a child's teddy bear, this animal is really not a bear at all. Rather, it's correctly identified as a marsupial. But that didn't prevent early taxonomists from making the association with bears. So the koala's scientific name, *Phascolarctos*, combines two Greek words: *phaskolos* (φάσκωλος), meaning 'pouch', and *arktos* (ἄρκτος), meaning 'bear'.

But honestly, why get so complicated? We can simply call this animal 'adorable'.

NAMING NATURE

RANGIFER TARANDUS

Caribou

Caribou – also known as reindeer – have long roamed the Arctic lands of the far north. In the polar regions of Norway, Finland, Sweden, Siberia, Greenland, Canada and Alaska, their herds can swell to as many as half a million animals. Those herds provide food, tools, clothing and revenue to the world's most northern Indigenous communities. (And if traditional tales are to be believed, they also give a boost to Santa Claus on Christmas Eve.)

In addition, caribou make one of the most impressive migrations in all of nature. I'll never forget being woken in the middle of a summer's night while camping in Alaska's Brooks Range. The ground under my sleeping bag started shaking – so vigorously I felt sure it was an earthquake – as a powerful rumble grew louder. But it wasn't a quake after all. It was a herd of caribou moving in unison across the tundra, as they have for ages. And I dearly hope that such migrations will continue for ages to come. While some of that fragile landscape is protected as parks and the Arctic National Wildlife Refuge, much of it could be destroyed by oil and gas development.

The names of these hardy creatures have travelled just as widely as their herds. The word 'caribou' originated with the Indigenous Mi'kmaq people, residents of what is now eastern Canada, who call the animals *qalipu*. That word refers to the animals' ability to dig in the snow with their hairy hooves to uncover edible plants such as willow shoots and lichens. Hundreds of years ago, French trappers and hunters in that region started using the Mi'kmaq word, and the name eventually morphed into 'caribou'.

Similarly, our modern word 'reindeer' probably came from the Old Norse name for the animal, *hreinn*. That word is related to *raingo*, long used by the Sámi people of northern Scandinavia.

c. 1600 | Anselmus de Boodt | *Rangifer*

Those sources led to the first word in the scientific term for the species, *Rangifer tarandus*.

The second word of this animal's scientific name, *tarandus*, came from mythology. It was the name of a legendary kind of deer that could change colours at will. That mythical deer, originally described in the writings of Aristotle and Pliny the Elder, has bounded through our collective imagination for over two thousand years.

Indigenous peoples in Arctic lands have their own unique names for these creatures. To the Athabaskans, they are *ʔekwǫ* or *tǫdzı* (depending on whether herds graze on the tundra or in the forest). To the Inuit people, they are *tuktu*. Among the Gwich'ins, whose traditional culture is deeply entwined with the caribou, they are often called *vadzaih*.

Several years ago, I was fortunate enough to witness the summer solstice festivities of the Gwich'in tribe, which took place north of the Arctic Circle. In a spectacular display of their longstanding connection with the caribou, people celebrated them in a wonderful array of songs, dances, garments, stories, carvings and blessings. While there, I learnt that the Gwich'in have more than twenty different names for caribou – emphasising the great importance of those animals to life as well as language.

MAGNIFICENT MAMMALS

CHLAMYPHORUS TRUNCATUS
Pink Fairy Armadillo

While not really a fairy, this highly elusive little creature is almost as difficult to find as a fairy queen or king. For the pink fairy armadillo is the world's tiniest kind of armadillo. Native to Argentina's desert region, it lives underground and only comes out at night to hunt for insects or worms.

In South America, it's known as *pichiciego*. That name combines *pichi*, the word in the Indigenous Araucanian language for 'small', and *ciego*, the Spanish term for 'blind' (based on colonists' incorrect assumption that these animals were sightless).

In Spanish, *armadillo* means 'little armoured one'. The ancient Aztecs, however, used a different name for these creatures, calling them *āyōtōchtli*, which is Nahuatl for 'turtle rabbit' (because of their turtle-like shell and rabbit-like fur). Meanwhile, in Portuguese, these animals are known as *tatu*, which came from the Tupi language spoken by Indigenous peoples in southern Brazil. The term combines the Tupian words for 'armour' and 'thick', and is used today in Brazil, Argentina and Bolivia. Another name used in parts of South America is *quirquincho*, which stems from the Quechuan word *kirkinchu*.

In addition to the pink fairy armadillo, there are several other varieties. Some of them have memorable (and entertaining) names, as well. There's the 'giant armadillo', the 'Chacoan naked-tailed armadillo' and the 'long-nosed armadillo'. There's even one called the 'big hairy armadillo'.

What is the pink fairy armadillo's champion survival skill? That might surprise you. This little animal can dig a hole and hide with amazing speed, thanks to its exceptional claws. In fact, some people call it by the nickname 'sand swimmer' because of its ability to dig so fast it can move through sand almost like water.

1842 | Charles Hamilton Smith | *Chlamyphorus truncatus*

Its most notable physical feature, of course, is the pink dorsal shell that covers its body (and which also ends so abruptly that it looks sawed off). The light rosy hue comes from blood vessels underneath the shell.

Most likely, this creature's name started out as 'pink fair armadillo'. Then, in the Victorian era of the late 1800s, 'fair' got changed to 'fairy'. Probably that happened because of the era's fascination with fairies, fairy realms and all things supernatural. As 'fairy creatures', they became highly prized by collectors and museums in Europe and North America.

Chlamyphorus truncatus is the scientific name for these little marvels. The first part, *Chlamyphorus*, refers to their shells, melding the Greek terms *chlamys* ('cloak') and *phorus* ('carrier'). The second part, *truncatus*, is Latin for 'cut off', to describe the shells' abrupt end.

While it's technically accurate, at least about the shell, the scientific name is not truly descriptive of this marvellous creature. This little animal, so delicate and elusive that it seems almost unworldly, surely deserves a more evocative name. It really ought to be called something with a bit of whimsy, a touch of wonder and perhaps . . . a sprinkle of magic from the fairy realms.

GIRAFFIDAE
Giraffe

One of the world's most impressive beings, the giraffe is strikingly tall, measuring up to 5.7 metres (19 feet). Thanks to its big legs and enormously long neck, it can reach amazingly high – a necessary skill to munch on the leaves of acacia trees.

That long neck, by the way, has just seven vertebrae, the same number as in the human neck. But each of the giraffe's vertebrae is much larger than ours. As a result, this creature can reach higher and see further than any other animal that keeps its feet on the ground.

Also equipped with a powerful heart to circulate blood through its body, an adult giraffe can run swiftly. Some have been recorded loping at 57 kilometres (35 miles) per hour. That's more than twice as fast as the average human can sprint. Surprisingly, even with such long legs, a female giraffe gives birth while standing. So she drops a newborn from a height of almost 2 metres (6 feet) – which gives that newborn a rather sudden entrance into the grasslands of Africa.

The name 'giraffe' comes from the Arabic *zarāfah* (زرافة), which means 'fast walker' – certainly an accurate description. That name itself might have originated with the ancient Somali word for these animals, *geri*.

Throughout Africa, giraffes have many beautiful names. The Maasai people call them *olmaaut*, *oloodo-kirragata* or *olchangito-oodo*. In Zulu, giraffes are called *indlulamithi*, which translates to 'taller than trees'. Rwandan people call them *agasumbashyamba*, which means 'the beautiful thing that is taller than the forest'. Kenya's Meru tribe refers to giraffes as *nchang'i*, meaning 'the tallest'. And in the Bemba language of Zambia, the name is *indya buluba*, 'the animal that eats the highest blooms'.

1826 | Philipp Jakob Cretzschmar | *Giraffidae*

The first scientific name for this unique creature, *Giraffa camelopardalis*, came from the Greek word *kamelopardalis* – a combination of the words for camel (because of its long neck) and leopard (because of its spots). Clearly, having seen nothing else truly like a giraffe, early observers were desperate to find some familiar comparisons.

Lovely collective nouns have been used to describe a group of giraffes. Some people call them 'a kaleidoscope', while others call them 'a tower'. My choice for the best group name, though, is 'a journey of giraffes'.

For many centuries, people across Africa have revered these creatures. In Botswana, they are known as *thutlhwa*, which translates as 'the honoured ones'. One Twiga story describes the giraffe's origins with reverence as well as humour (and also explains why another African animal, the rhino, seems so perpetually grumpy). African cave paintings from long ago show giraffes standing tall. Ancient Egyptian hieroglyphics praised giraffes as the first creatures to see any changes in the distant landscape.

Given this longstanding admiration, it's hard to believe that the numbers of giraffes are declining in many countries. That's caused by the steady loss of their natural habitat. Yet surely we can find ways to help these extraordinary creatures survive. It's worth reaching very high indeed to save them.

SAGUINUS IMPERATOR
Emperor Tamarin

Whether or not the famous Kaiser Wilhelm would approve – and he probably would not – his long moustache inspired the name of this magnificent South American monkey. The emperor tamarin is an energetic, playful resident of tropical forests in Brazil, Bolivia and Peru. It's celebrated by animal lovers around the world, a prime ambassador of the Amazon region's rich biodiversity.

Yet its name originated from the simple fact of its enormous white moustache. Swiss-Brazilian naturalist Émil August Göldi mockingly compared it to the similarly long moustache of German Emperor Wilhelm II – and the name 'emperor' stuck.

What's the evolutionary purpose of such a prominent moustache? Because several different tamarin species may inhabit the same region, wildlife biologists believe those whiskers could help emperor tamarins find one another. They need to identify members of their own species in order to mate.

Both male and female emperor tamarins grow moustaches. So do young ones, sporting their own mini moustaches. While a troop of these monkeys will include males as well as females, the leader of the troop will always be the eldest female. She will reign over all the rest. Other varieties of tamarins have their own highly descriptive names. They're called 'mottle-faced', 'red-capped' and 'golden-handed'. And they're also known as 'white-lipped', 'black-handed' and 'cotton-topped'. Yet none of those names, it's fair to say, has quite the appeal of 'emperor'.

Even the monkey's scientific name, *Saguinus imperator*, reflects that royal connection. While the first part of the Latin name means 'monkey like a squirrel', the second part means 'emperor'. So people continue to celebrate this creature's resemblance to a certain historical figure – or, at least, to his moustache.

PROCYON LOTOR

Raccoon

Ever seen the paw of a raccoon? With long, flexible fingers, it closely resembles a human hand – so much that whenever I see a raccoon, I want to wave my own hand in greeting. Raccoons' fingers are extremely nimble, as well as highly sensitive – all of which helps them to find their food by touch. Not only that, those paws are so dexterous they can perform some very skilled moves. Raccoons can untie knots, turn doorknobs, lift latches and break into containers. They can seek out food efficiently at night. They can even open jars, especially if there's something tasty inside.

It's no surprise, then, that those paws inspired the very name 'raccoon'. The word originated with the Indigenous American Powhatan tribe. They called these creatures *aroughcun*, which translates as 'animal that scratches with its hands'.

The scientific name for raccoons also gives a nod to those capable mitts. That name, *Procyon lotor*, is Latin for 'before-dog washer'. The first part was included when early observers guessed that these animals were related to canines. But they're not – instead, they're related to badgers and otters. The 'washer' part of their name, though, is accurate. It refers to raccoons' common practice of dunking their paws, as well as their food, in water. The reason for this behaviour is to enhance their tactile sense, because they've learnt that dipping their paws into water makes the nerves even more sensitive.

1845 | James Audubon | *Procyon lotor*

The three collective terms for raccoons focus on different aspects of these creatures. 'A nursery of raccoons' was probably inspired by the sight of their cosy dens. Family groups, with up to seven offspring (called 'kits'), will stay huddled inside hollow trees for several weeks in springtime. Eventually, they will go out and forage together, under the watchful eyes of their mother. Another collective term is 'a gaze of raccoons'. The origin of this one is more difficult to explain. Maybe it arose from raccoons' habit of standing on their rear legs to gaze at something that's caught their attention. Or maybe it came from their tendency to stare into a source of light at night, which you've surely noticed if you've gone outside with a torch and found them. The last collective term was inspired by raccoons' unusual markings around their eyes. Only applied to a group of males, such groups are called 'a mask of raccoons'.

An Encounter with a Mountain Gorilla

Dawn's first light filtered through the tall groves of bamboo in Rwanda's Volcanoes National Park – a spectacular gem in Central Africa. The wet toes of my hiking boots glistened as we climbed higher up the ridge of Karisimbi, at almost 4,507 metres (15,000 feet), the highest peak in the Virunga range.

Led by our local guide, Nsenge, an experienced tracker who had grown up in neighbouring Congo, we pushed through the dense bamboo. At last, he signalled us to move slowly. Hearts pounding, we cautiously approached a group of gorillas. We sat in a spot strewn with bamboo leaves, just far enough away to watch the unfolding drama without disrupting it.

And what a drama! More than twenty of those powerful creatures filled the grove, gorillas of all ages, sizes and personalities. Young toddlers, full of mischief, strode around, tumbling over themselves, chasing one another, sometimes climbing on top of a dozing elder. Adolescents wrestled in the bamboo and beat their chests loudly. A sturdy mother with thick brown fur held a youngster in her arms. An enormous silverback sat apart, chewing on a bamboo shoot, as he watched over the group.

Then I noticed, across the grove, a young mother gorilla nursing her infant. Her deep brown eyes met mine, and for a long while, we gazed at each other. I could feel, in those eyes, her warmth and devotion to her child. And I could also feel her trust, allowing us to enter her family circle.

All of a sudden – a big silverback, weighing at least 180 kilogrammes (400 pounds), crashed through the bamboo right behind us. Grunting, he lumbered directly towards my back. Quickly I slid sideways to open a pathway for him to pass through and join the rest of his group. But when he reached me, he did something completely unexpected. He sat his great bulk down on the leaves right beside me!

The mountain gorilla leant sideways, pushing his massive shoulder right into mine. Though my heart raced, I tried to keep utterly still. He leant further, pressing his bulk against me. Clearly, he was sending me a message. *This is my family, human. You can watch, but you'd better behave . . . or else.*

Eventually, he rose. With a final grunt, he lumbered over to join the others.

Years later, I can still feel that gorilla's hefty shoulder leaning against mine. Still hear his gusty breathing. And still see, across the bamboo grove, the young mother's deep brown eyes.

1897 | E. Lloyd | *Gorilla*

CHAPTER 8

Creatures Fabulous and Frightening

Speak again, spider!

It is hard to hear your words

in the autumn gale.

MATSUO BASHO, TRANSLATED FROM THE JAPANESE

NOCTILUCA SCINTILLANS

Bioluminescent Algae

One of my favourite names of bioluminescent algae is *Noctiluca*, which is Latin for 'night light'. If you've ever been at the seashore and seen glowing light in the waves, it's probably from these microscopic creatures. Their most common nicknames are 'fire algae', 'sea ghosts' and – my top choice – 'sea sparkle'.

One marvellous legend, from the Indigenous people of the Kiribati islands in the Pacific, explained how fire came to humans. To those oceanic people, it originated not from lightning but rather from the sparkling light of the sea.

'Bioluminescent' means, literally, 'life that makes light'. Consider how amazing that is: living beings, like ourselves, which have the ability to produce their own light – akin to a flaming tree, a bolt of lightning or a distant supernova. But in this case, the light is created by living organisms that make light through chemical reactions inside themselves, combining luciferin molecules and enzymes to kindle a special kind of fire.

On land, only a few kinds of creatures can produce light. Fireflies and glowworms are the most well known. Certain mushrooms can also do it, including one with a purple top that has the lovely name 'lilac bonnet' and another that bears the alluring label 'eternal light mushroom'.

In the ocean, however, this ability is much more widespread. Way down in the deepest waters, where no light from the surface can ever reach, most creatures carry their own 'torches'. Those luminous beings range from the infinitesimally small bioluminescent algae to the Pacific Ocean's Humboldt squid, which can reach over 2 metres (almost 7 feet) long. They also include the otherworldly lanternfish with their huge, round eyes, as well as the firefly squid, called *hotaru-ika* in Japan, which converge on Toyama Bay every spring and fill the bay with eerie blue light.

Whether the light produced by these creatures is blue, green, red or yellow, it's always because of the chemical reaction within themselves. As a result, they have the power – quite literally – to light up their world.

LEPAS ANATIFERA

Gooseneck Barnacle

Living in the open ocean, gooseneck barnacles attach themselves to floating driftwood and ride the waves while feeding on plankton. As hermaphrodites, with both male and female body parts, these crustaceans produce larvae that swim freely until they, too, find a convenient ship to ride. But as remarkable as their lives at sea may be, the legends about gooseneck barnacles are far more remarkable – and those legends still swirl around them like ocean currents.

Back in the early days of Britain, people wondered why a type of black goose, commonly seen near coastlines in winter, seemed to disappear every summer – and then somehow reappear the next winter. Unaware of the birds' annual migration to breed in the Arctic, folk pointed to the coastal driftwood covered with barnacles that eerily resembled the shape and colour of those missing geese, with long necks, beaked heads and maybe even folded wings. Could they be connected?

Along came an English monk in the eighth century, the Venerable Bede. He described a kind of goose that grew on driftwood from the ocean. People started to wonder . . . might those geese have emerged from seawater by spontaneous generation? In the twelfth century, the archdeacon Gerald of Wales made that very claim in *Topographia Hibernica*, which included his own description of the baby geese he had seen growing on scraps of driftwood. These barnacle geese, he postulated, were 'neither flesh, nor born

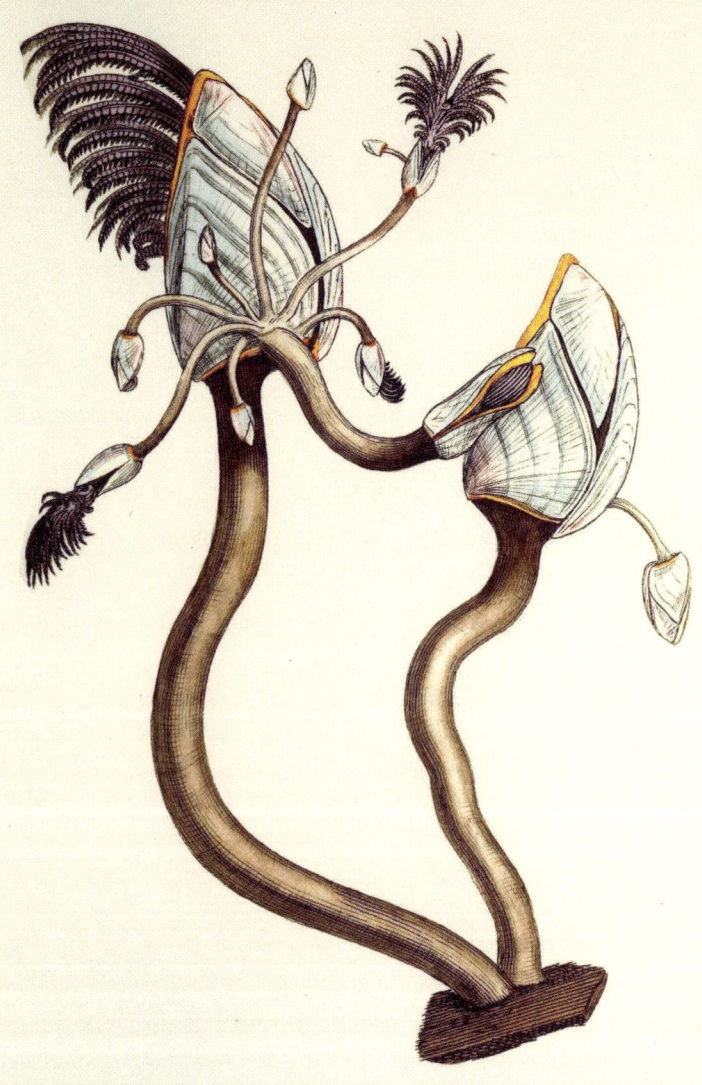

1815 | William Wood | *Lepas anatifera*

of flesh'. Seizing on that notion, some churches decreed that during Meatless Fridays and Lent, people could eat the birds that presumably came from those barnacles, because they were actually a kind of fish.

Ultimately, though, sceptics found all this just too much to swallow. In 1241, Holy Roman Emperor Frederick II dispatched special envoys to study these mythical creatures, and concluded the tales were merely superstition. Two centuries later, Pope Pius II made the same assessment when he met with the King of Scotland. Barnacles were barnacles; geese were geese.

Yet legends persisted of those miraculous creatures born spontaneously at sea – even among scientifically minded people. As late as 1661, the first president of the Royal Society, Sir Robert Moray, reported that he had seen some splendidly formed geese inside the shells of barnacles. Up to the late eighteenth century, people made similar claims.

But let's not laugh too hard. Though they were woefully unscientific, those people who celebrated the miracle of barnacle geese were inspired by the idea that the wonders of nature also have deeper spiritual meaning. They saw, in this flawed example, reminders of the power of metamorphosis, the limits of knowledge and the greatest miracle of all: creation.

And so, from every angle, the story of this name is a parable of our deep yearning to understand the world, and our imperfect attempts to do so. It's also a reminder of the value of humility. After all . . . we humans ourselves are just tiny barnacles, cast adrift, floating for a while on the vast and mysterious sea of life.

STOMATOPODA

Mantis Shrimp

When we humans look at the world through our highly evolved eyes, we can perceive colours through three channels – blue, green and red. For the mantis shrimp, which has the most complex eyes of any animal on the planet, that's just a drop in an ocean-sized bucket.

With its compound eyes attached to stalks, each of which holds thousands of ommatidia photoreceptors, it can view twelve distinct channels of colour. That's right – twelve. And it can also perceive both ultraviolet light and polarised light. While scientists disagree over how well a mantis shrimp can distinguish between the kaleidoscopic array of possible colours, there's no question that this little marine crustacean is perceiving the world in ways we can barely even imagine.

Found throughout the Pacific and Indian Oceans, these animals have many names in many tongues. Some of those names are pejorative because of the mantis shrimp's dangerous claws and ability to spear or smash their prey (or any unlucky person who touches them). For that reason, Australians call them 'thumb splitters'. Brazilians call them *siriboia*, which combines two Indigenous words – *si'ri*, meaning 'crab', and *mboi*, meaning 'serpent'. And Assyrians of ancient times derided them as 'sea locusts'. By contrast, to the people of French Polynesia, who know them by the Tahitian word *varo*, they're prized as delicious food.

The name mantis arises from the Greek term *mantikos* (μαντικός), meaning 'prophet'. But unlike the famous insect, the praying mantis, which was so named because of its distinctive prayerful stance, these crustaceans were named because of the similarity of their forelimbs to those of the insect. Both are small but fearsome predators, capable of using those forelimbs to seize and grasp their next meal.

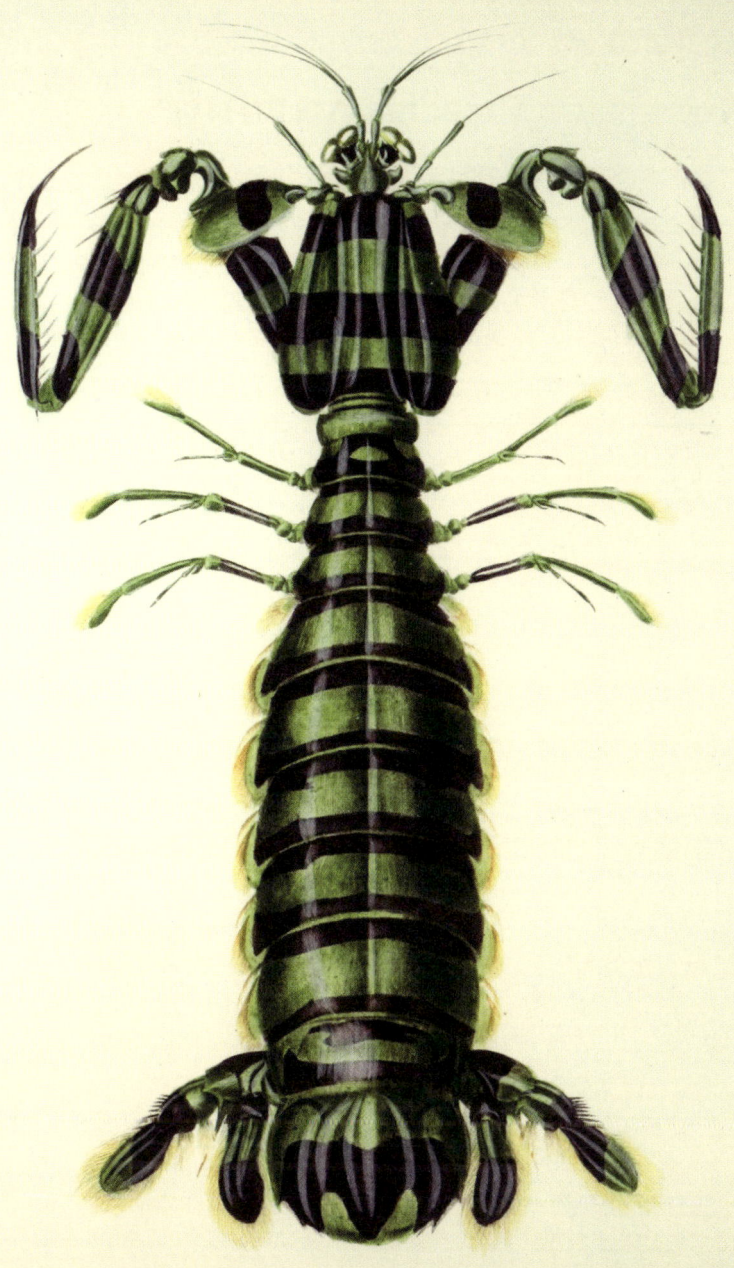

1896 | Richard Lydekker | *Stomatopoda*

Perhaps the most surprising name for a variety of mantis shrimp was given to an extinct genus that lived long ago in the Mesozoic era. Scientists called it *Sculda*, after Skuld, one of the three mythical Norse goddesses of fate. Legends tell of them seated eternally beneath the great tree Yggdrasil, weaving the threads of life, death and destiny. Perhaps those mythical goddesses were also perceiving the world with an endless kaleidoscope of colours?

People have given many other memorable labels to the modern kinds of mantis shrimp. Various species have been dubbed 'zebra', 'peacock', 'orange spot' and 'harlequin' (which dines exclusively on starfish). Others are named 'striped', 'painted', 'clown' and 'white tiger'. And there's even one called 'rainbow'. Colourful names, indeed.

WUNDERPUS PHOTOGENICUS

Wunderpus Octopus

Many are the reasons to admire the octopus. (I can think of at least eight.) Start with their great intelligence. With the biggest brain relative to body size of any creature without a spinal column, an octopus can solve mazes, remember encounters, taste as well as feel with its suckers and even use tools. That's right – an octopus can wield tools to get food, defend itself or clear away debris.

In addition, different kinds of octopus have the ability to stretch themselves out to huge dimensions or shrink down to very small sizes. They can squirt black ink at any attackers. And if that's not sufficient to avoid trouble, they can also camouflage themselves by dramatically changing the colours of their skin.

1851 | A. E. d'Audebard Férussac | *Octopus vulgaris*

The word 'octopus' originated from the Greek term *oktōpous*, meaning 'eight foot', combining *oktō*, 'eight', with *pous*, 'foot'. Some people call a group of these creatures 'a consortium'. But to me, a much more delightful collective term for them is 'a tangle of octopuses'. Imagine a gathering where so many arms and tentacles are curling around each other that everyone is, indeed, part of 'a tangle'.

Many kinds of octopus have inspired evocative names. The 'dumbo octopus' has fins that look like rounded ears. The 'flapjack octopus' can make itself look as flat as a ... well, you know. The 'blanket octopus' floats through the water, looking very much like a wet blanket. The 'pygmy octopus' is very small. The 'coconut octopus' carries a coconut shell to use as a hiding place if needed. The 'mimic octopus' can disguise itself to look like a crab, a sea snake or even a jellyfish.

Among these spectacularly capable creatures, one of the most amazing varieties is the wunderpus. Named for the German word *wunder*, which means 'marvel', this octopus is worthy of admiration, even astonishment. As such, it's a popular subject for photographers and video makers. So much so, its scientific name is *Wunderpus photogenicus*.

This beautifully coloured master of disguise can instantly change itself to imitate predators. A wunderpus can shape-shift to look like a poisonous lionfish, complete with long and lethal spines. Or it can swiftly take the form of a dangerous sea snake. A wunderpus has been seen to hide six of its arms, making sure they can't be noticed, while undulating the other two arms just like banded sea snakes.

That's not all the tricks up its many sleeves. A wunderpus can simply shift colours – so effectively that it virtually disappears into its surroundings. Or in a pinch, the wunderpus can actually lose one of its own arms to evade a predator – and then later regrow the missing limb. How's that for a marvel?

RUSAVSKIA ELEGANS
Elegant Sunburst Lichen

With the striking orange and gold colours of sunrise, as well as exceptional sturdiness in very difficult conditions, this lichen is one of nature's most remarkable life forms. Its beauty and its grace under pressure are so well balanced that it truly deserves the name 'elegant'.

Like all lichens, the elegant sunburst lichen is a symbiotic combination of alga and fungus, with the alga making food through photosynthesis and the fungus giving stability to the organism. This particular lichen thrives in many diverse environments around the world, even at very high altitudes on the mountain ridges of the Himalayas. Known to scientists as *Rusavskia elegans*, it's both hardy enough to survive Siberian winters and beautiful enough to be celebrated for its colour.

That bright orange colour is actually a key to its extraordinary hardiness. For that colour, which comes from anthraquinone pigments in its cortex, is also a natural sunscreen. It protects the organism effectively from ultraviolet rays and other harmful sorts of radiation. How effectively? A few years ago, the elegant sunburst lichen was chosen for an important scientific study. A clump was transported all the way out to the International Space Station. Then it was left in the vacuum of space, unprotected against great extremes of temperature and radioactivity, for over a year. Miraculously, the lichen survived – the ultimate in sheer durability.

How ironic, then, that this hardy life form is also very sensitive to air pollution. While it can withstand the extremes of outer space, it can't survive bad air. So in a surprising twist, it represents both the great sturdiness and the great vulnerability of life on Earth.

VELELLA VELELLA
By-the-Wind Sailor

Never has a life form been more aptly named. Resembling a kind of scallop or mussel that rides the ocean waves, keeping its shell erect as a sail, these creatures move around entirely *by the wind*.

Also called 'sea rafts', some have sails that are angled to the left of prevailing winds, while others are angled to the right. That's more than just a genetic variation – it's how these creatures have managed to disperse across vast stretches of the oceans.

In Italy, where the language often seems more akin to music than words, one of these creatures would be called *la barchetta di San Pietro*. That lilting phrase means 'the small boat of Saint Peter'. Long ago, in Italian rural tradition, the appearance of these 'boats' along the shore was a favourable sign for the coming harvest.

The scientific name for these creatures is also highly descriptive – as well as rather musical to say aloud. *Velella velella* they are called, which means 'small sail' in Latin. Cicero, the Roman philosopher, used the word in that very context. At some point in their voyages across the oceans of language, these words probably sailed on the same linguistic boat as the Sanskrit term *vah*, meaning 'to carry'.

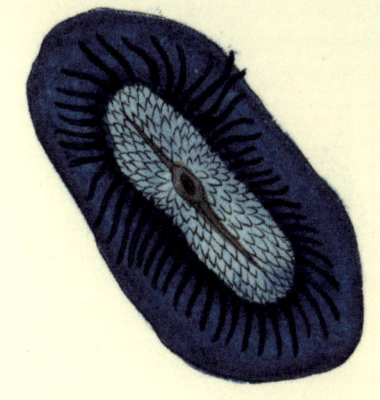
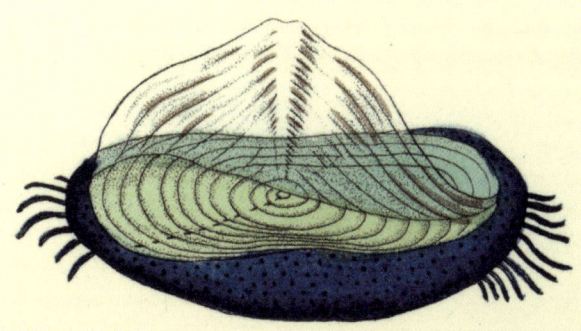

1796 | George Shaw | *Velella velella*

In fact, these intrepid sailors aren't really scallops or mussels, but hydrozoans, which are related to jellyfish. What appears to be one organism is actually a whole colony of hydrozoans. They work together to catch plankton, digest food, reproduce at sea – and of course, like good sailors, keep the sail hoisted at all times. Together, they function much like a sailing ship, with crewmates who do everything from swabbing the decks to preparing the meals to repairing the sails.

That's how these evocatively named life forms have survived so well for over 300 million years. Today, they continue to ride the high seas, voyaging wherever the winds may take them.

◇◇◇◇◇◇◇◇◇◇◇◇◇◇◇

THERAPHOSA BLONDI

Goliath Bird-Eating Tarantula

Hidden in the rainforests of Venezuela, Guyana and Brazil, a rather frightening creature lives in dark, silk-padded burrows, emerging only after nightfall. The Goliath bird-eating tarantula is, in body mass, the biggest spider on Earth. Typically, it grows to a body length of over 13 centimetres (5 inches) and leg length of more than twice that, with thick hair covering everything.

That's not the most frightening part. This cuddly little creature eats by capturing its prey, then liquefying the prey's internal organs. And then, over time, it will drain away the contents – savouring every last drop – until there's nothing left but an empty sack.

1705 | Maria Sibylla Merian | *Theraphosa blondi*

Small wonder that the scientific name of the genus of this spider is *Theraphosa*. That word is derived from the Ancient Greek term *thēr* (θήρ), meaning 'beast' or 'monster'.

Before we look closely at the name 'Goliath bird-eating tarantula', it's worth noting that there are many different kinds of tarantula, some of which also have memorable names. There's one called the 'Malaysian earthtiger', another called the 'peacock' and yet another called the 'blue-fang skeleton', a terrifying name if there ever was one. Others are called 'Togo starburst baboon' and 'Mexican blood leg'. Yet the name 'Goliath bird-eating tarantula' combines widely diverse sources like no other.

The first part of the spider's name, 'Goliath', springs from the biblical story of David and Goliath and is clearly intended to convey the spider's gigantic size as well as the terrifying sight of this huge attacker. In Hebrew, the name Goliath is derived from *golyāth*, which is related to the verb *gala* (הלג), meaning 'to go into exile'.

What about the second part of the name, 'bird-eating'? That most likely originated with an engraving made three hundred years ago by the talented German naturalist and entomologist Maria Sibylla Merian. In that celebrated engraving, she depicted a tarantula busily chowing down on a hummingbird.

The third part of the name, 'tarantula', has its own unique story, with a surprising plot, intriguing characters and a lingering touch of mystery. The word originated in the town of Taranto, Italy, where another hairy spider, *Lycosa tarantula*, was first identified sometime in the fourteenth century. The bite of that spider was once believed to cause a strange disease, tarantism, with symptoms that included weeping and delirium, unusual sexual desires and wild dancing. Tarantism appeared in southern Italy, grew into an extraordinary dancing mania and lasted into the seventeenth century. Today, a milder form of it continues in a wonderfully energetic folk dance called the tarantella (commonly called 'dance of the spider').

Although we can't know for sure how the original mania of tarantism began, it most likely had psychological and social roots, not physical ones. Rather than being caused by the bite of a spider, it arose, instead, from the bite of the human condition.

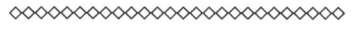

VAMPYROTEUTHIS INFERNALIS

Vampire Squid

'Vampire squid from hell'. That's the precise translation of this animal's scientific name, *Vampyroteuthis infernalis*. Not many creatures carry a name that is so loaded down with negative baggage. We all understand the meaning of 'vampire', long used to describe a terrifying being of the shadows who just can't resist drinking the blood of humans. The English word grew out of the Hungarian term *vampir*, which itself evolved from the Slavonic term *qpyri*. And of course, the word 'hell' isn't exactly the name of a lovely place to visit (although you could say it's a destination of sorts). That word is derived from the Old Norse word *hel*, meaning 'place of the dead', which evolved to the Old German *hellia*, and ultimately, to the English word we use today.

First described in 1903 by German marine biologist Carl Chun, the vampire squid isn't, in fact, a squid. Nor is it an octopus, though it shares some similarities. It's the lone surviving member of the taxonomic order of a distant relative of the octopus, a 'living fossil' cephalopod whose ancestry stretches back more than 100 million years.

What inspired such a thoroughly demonic name? For starters, this creature lives in the deepest, darkest realms of the ocean. Not only does it have the scary, cloaked appearance of all squid, its overall colour is dark, bloody red. And its eyes are so swollen they're the biggest in proportion to the body of any animal on the planet. Oh, and let's not forget to mention its eerie bioluminescence, which can cast wavering light even in the most shadowy depths. In addition, it can spray globs of glowing mucus that can stick to the body of any attacker.

Beyond question, all these characteristics are helpful to the vampire squid's survival in the remote undersea zones where it lives. And equally beyond question, they amount to one terrifying, demonic creature – one that is scary as hell.

1920 | Albert I, Prince of Monaco | *Vampyroteuthis infernalis*

An Encounter with a Giant Pacific Octopus

This was a date I had long awaited. Not a date with another human. Rather, this was a date to meet an octopus. And not just any octopus, but a giant Pacific octopus – the largest kind of octopus in the world.

By the good graces of Sally, a friend at California's Monterey Bay Aquarium, I'd been granted permission to venture behind the scenes, to the specialised tanks reserved for close observation. Sally and I finally arrived at one especially large tank. She opened the top, revealing a magnificent creature, moving swiftly and gracefully across the tank's glass wall towards us. A giant Pacific octopus.

My heart raced. You see, for my whole life, I've loved octopuses. The way they move, the way they look, the way they think. The more I learnt about them, the more fascinated I became, admiring their shape-shifting abilities, their incredible skill in camouflage and most of all, their intelligence.

The octopus reached our side of the tank. Reddish pink in colour, with eight fluid arms, she grasped the upper rim of the glass wall and peered at us. While she had the ability to expand her size greatly – she could stretch her arms as long as a pick-up truck – she was currently keeping herself small. With a nod from Sally, I rolled up the sleeve

of my shirt and plunged my arm into the
cold seawater.

    Instantly, the tank churned and splashed, spraying me from head to toe. A long, flexible arm swiftly gripped me, wrapping itself around my forearm, elbow and bicep. Not too tightly, just enough to be sure I would stay for a while. Meanwhile, suckers gently caressed my skin – a strange yet beautiful sensation. I knew this octopus had more than two thousand suckers on her eight arms, each of which held highly capable sensors allowing her to simultaneously touch, smell, and taste my body. This may have been our first date . . . but it was quickly getting intimate.

    The octopus's otherworldly eyes studied me. I had the distinct feeling that this wondrous creature was just as interested in me as I was in her.

    When the time came to leave, I took hold of her arm and gently started to pull her away from my skin. She resisted, clinging tight, even trying to grab me with another arm. Eventually, though, she relented. I heard a series of loud pops, like dozens of bubbles bursting, as the suckers released. Swiftly, she drew away and slipped back into the water.

    Though I never saw her again, it was a date I will always cherish.

Index

A

albatrosses (*Diomedeidae*) 29–31
alerce (*Fitzroya cupressoides*) 100–2
algae *see bioluminiscent algae*
Amazon 40, 44, 64, 65, 126, 168, 172, 181, 219
Amazon pink dolphins (*Inia geoffrensis*) 64–5
American woodcocks *see timberdoodles*
amphibians 164–87
axolotls (*Ambystoma mexcanum*) 183–4
Aztecs 20, 27, 184, 213

B

baby tooth mosses (*Plagiomnium cuspidatum*) 105–6
bioluminescent algae (*Noctiluca scintillans*) 230–1
birds 16–53
birds of paradise (*Strelitzia reginae*) 90–2
blackbirds 46
boobooks 39
bowerbirds (*Archboldia papuensis*) 32–5
by-the-wind sailors (*Velella velella*) 240–2

C

camouflage 59, 140–63, 236, 248
caribous (*Rangifer tarandus*) 210–12
Celtic 39, 43, 93
chimpanzees (*Pan troglodytes*) 204–6
coast redwoods (*Sequoia sempervirens*) 96–8, 114–15
crane flowers *see Birds of Paradise*
cuckoos 39

D

Darwin 69
dawn redwood 97
diatoms (*Bacillariophyceae*) 150–2
dolphins 64–5, 147
dragonflies (*Anisoptera*) 120–22
dugongs (*Dugong dugon*) 195–7

E

electric eels (*Electrophorus electricus*) 168–9
elegant sunburst lichens (*Rusavskia elegans*) 239
elephant head flowers (*Pedicularis groenlandica*) 103–5
elephants (*Elephantidae*) 198–200
emerald tree boas (*Corallus caninus*) 178–9

emperor tamarins (*Saguinus imperator*) 219
eucalyptuses 88–9
  balsam trees 89
  rainbow eucalyptuses (*Eucalyptus deglupta*) 88–9
  tepa trees 89

F

fireflies (*Lampyridae*) 130–1
foxgloves (*Digitalis purpurea*) 92–4

G

Galápagos 68–9, 144, 172, 174, 186–7
ghost crabs (*Ocypodidae*) 144–6
giant Pacific octopuses 248–9
giant sequoia 97
giraffes (*Giraffidae*) 216–18
goblin sharks (*Mitsukiurina owstoni*) 58–9
goldcrests (*Regulus regulus*) 35–7
goliath bird-eating tarantulas (*Theraphosa blondi*) 242–5
gooseneck barnacles (*Lepas anatifera*) 231–3
grasses of Parnassus (*Parnassia palustris*) 110–11

H

halcyon birds (*Alcedinidae*) 24–7
hellbenders (*Cryptobranchus alleganiensis*) 175–7
huet-huets (*Pteroptochos tarnii*) 37–9
hummingbirds (*Trochilidae*) 27–8
  bee hummingbird 28
humpback whales (*Megaptera novaeangliae*) 70–2
humuhumunukunukuapua'as (*Rhinecanthus rectangulus*) 73–4

I

Indigenous Americans 22
  Abenaki 51
  Blackfoot 105, 152
  Cherokee 130
  Cheyenne 22, 105
  Cree 51, 152
  Dakota 153
  Hopi 47
  Inupiat 46
  Lakota Sioux 22
  Mapuche 47, 89, 102

INDEX

Miwok 98
Navajo 120
Northern Chipewyan 152
Ojibwa 105, 130
Powhatan Renape 100, 220
Yup'ik 46
Yurok 98
Zunis 122
Indigenous Australians
  Gugadja 158
  Noongar Boodjar 61
  Pintupi 158
  Warlpiri 158
  Wiradjuri 35
  Yuin-Kurik 39
insects 116–39

J

jellyfish (*Cinidaria*) 66–8
  lion's mane 66
  moon jellies (*Aurelia aurita*) 66–8

K

kiss-me-over-the-garden-gate (*Persicaria orientalis*) 112–13
koalas (*Phascolarctos cinereus*) 207–9

L

languages
  Afrikaans 135
  Ancient Persian 90
  Arabic 30, 152, 158, 216
  Balinese 129
  Basque 28
  Bemba 216
  Chinese 74, 129
  Croatian 120
  Czech 28
  Danish 106
  Dutch 30, 68, 129
  Finnish 129
  French 24, 43, 90, 106, 120, 128, 137, 155, 157, 198
  Gaelic 93, 122
  German 29, 43, 68, 77, 90, 106, 128, 135, 146
  Hawai'ian 70, 72, 73–4, 129, 144
  Hindi 129, 156
  Hungarian 106, 137
  Inuktitut 148
  Italian 90, 106, 129, 240
  Japanese 58, 129, 134
  Laotian 171
  Lithuanian 106
  Nahuatl 20
  Namibian 126
  Norse 106
  Norwegian 35, 129
  Old English 32, 106, 146
  Old French 43
  Old German 32, 43, 169, 245
  Old Norse 245
  Polish 28
  Portuguese 40, 64, 90, 129, 135, 213
  Russian 68, 128, 135
  Slovenian 171
  Spanish 28, 37, 40, 64, 90, 102, 106, 128, 144, 213
  Swahili 171
  Taíno 28
  Tok Pisin 171
  Tupian 168, 213
  Turkish 137
  Welsh 43, 129
  Zulu 216
lauwiliwilinukunuku'oi'oi 74
leafy sea dragons (*Phycodurus eques*) 59–61
luna moths (*Actias luna*) 132–4, 138–9

M

Maasai 216
Madagascan sunset moths (*Chrysiridia hipheus*) 123–5
maidenhair ferns (*Adiantum capillus-veneris*) 107–9
mammals 188–225
mantis shrimp (*Stomatopoda*) 234–6
Māori 72
marine iguanas (*Amblyrhynchus cristatus*) 172–4, 186–7
meadowlarks (*Sturnella neglecta*) 22–4
merlins (*Falco columbarius*) 42–4
methuselah's beard lichens (*Dolichousnea longissima*) 152–4
moonflowers (*Ipomoea alba*) 94–6
morpho butterflies (*Nymphalidae*) 126–9
mountain gorillas 223–5

N

Namib desert beetles (*Stenocara gracilipes*) 125–6
nudibranchs (*Chromodorididae*) 61–3
    Loch's chromodoris slug (*Chromodoris lochi*) 62
    Spanish dancer (*Hexabranchus sanguineus*) 62

O

orchids
    calypso (*Calypso bulbosa*) 86
    dragon's mouth (*Arethusa bulbosa*) 86–8
organ pipe corals (*Tubipora musica*) 74–6
owls 39

P

passerines 39
pilmaiquen *see swallows*
pink fairy armadillos (*Chlamyphorus trucantus*) 213–15
pinocchio frogs (*Litoria Pinocchio*) 170–1
platypuses (*Ornithorhynchus anatinus*) 201–3
Pliny the Elder 66, 107, 178, 212
poison dart frogs (*Dendrobatidae*) 181–2
praying mantises (*Mantidea*) 135–7
predicted antwrens (*Herpsilochmus praedictus*) 44–5
pumpkin toadlets (*Brachycephalus ephippium*) 185

R

raccoons (*Procyonidae*) 220–3
red-lipped batfish (*Ogcocephalus darwini*) 68–9
redwood trees *see coast redwoods*
reef triggerfish *see humuhumunukunukuapua'as*
resplendent quetzals (*Pharomachrus mocinno*) 20–2

S

sandhill cranes 52–3
sarcastic fringeheads (*Neoclinus blanchardi*) 78–9
Sasquatches *see yetis*
screaming pihas (*Lipaugus vociferans*) 40–1
sea butterflies (*Thecosomata*) 77–8
sempervirens (*Sequoia sempervirens*) 96–8
snow leopards (*Panthera uncia*) 154–6, 162–31
spirit bears (*Ursus americanus kermodei*) 192–4
swallows (*Hirundinidae*) 47–9

T

timberdoodles (*Scolopax minor*) 50–1
truffles (*Tuberaceae*) 157–9

U

unicorns of the sea (*Monodon monoceros*) 147–9

V

vampire squid (*Vampyroteuthis infernalis*) 245–7
venus flytraps (*Dionaea muscipula*) 98–100

W

water animals 54–81
water ouzels (*Cinclus mexicanus*) 45–6
whales 70–2, 80–1
woodpeckers 39
wunderpus octopuses (*Wunderpus photogenicus*) 236–8

Y

yetis 160–1

Credits

The publisher would like to thank the following for their permission to reproduce material:

PICTURE CREDITS:

2: RawPixel/Rijksmuseum, 21: Flickr/Biodiversity Heritage Library, 23: Flickr/Biodiversity Heritage Library, 25: Flickr/Biodiversity Heritage Library, 26: Digital Bodleian/Bodleian Libraries, University of Oxford, 29: Bridgeman/Brown Bear/Windmill/Universal Images Group, 33: Bridgeman/Edinburgh University Library, 34: The New York Public Library/General Research Division, 38: Flickr/Biodiversity Heritage Library, 41: Bridgeman/Florilegius, 42: Flickr/Biodiversity Heritage Library, 49: Flickr/Biodiversity Heritage Library, 50: Bridgeman/Florilegius, 58: Flickr/Biodiversity Heritage Library, 60: Flickr/Biodiversity Heritage Library, 63: Bridgeman/Purix Verlag Volker Christen, 64: Bridgeman/British Library Archive, 67: Flickr/Biodiversity Heritage Library, 71: Flickr/Biodiversity Heritage Library, 73: Flickr/Biodiversity Heritage Library, 75: Bridgeman/Purix Verlag Volker Christen, 79: University of Washington/Freshwater and Marine Image Bank, 87: Flickr/Biodiversity Heritage Library, 91: Flickr/Biodiversity Heritage Library, 92: Flickr/Biodiversity Heritage Library, 95: Flickr/Biodiversity Heritage Library, 99: Flickr/Biodiversity Heritage Library, 101: Flickr/Biodiversity Heritage Library, 104: Flickr/Biodiversity Heritage Library, 109: Flickr/Biodiversity Heritage Library, 110: Flickr/Biodiversity Heritage Library, 113: Bridgeman/Florilegius, 121: Flickr/Biodiversity Heritage Library, 124: Flickr/Biodiversity Heritage Library, 127: Flickr/Biodiversity Heritage Library, 133: Flickr/Biodiversity Heritage Library, 136: Flickr/Biodiversity Heritage Library, 145: Flickr/Biodiversity Heritage Library, 147: Flickr/Biodiversity Heritage Library, 150: Flickr/Biodiversity Heritage Library, 155: Artvee, 157: Flickr/Biodiversity Heritage Library, 169: Flickr/Biodiversity Heritage Library, 173: Flickr/Biodiversity Heritage Library, 175: Wikimedia/Iconographia Zoologica, 179: Flickr/Biodiversity Heritage Library, 180: Flickr/Biodiversity Heritage Library, 183: Flickr/Biodiversity Heritage Library, 193: Artvee, 196: Flickr/Biodiversity Heritage Library, 199: Flickr/Biodiversity Heritage Library, 201: Flickr/Biodiversity Heritage Library, 205: Flickr/Biodiversity Heritage Library, 208: Flickr/Biodiversity Heritage Library, 211: Artvee, 214: Flickr/Biodiversity Heritage Library, 217: Flickr/Biodiversity Heritage Library, 221: Flickr/Biodiversity Heritage Library, 225: Flickr/Biodiversity Heritage Library, 232: Flickr/Biodiversity Heritage Library, 235: Flickr/Biodiversity Heritage Library, 237: Flickr/Biodiversity Heritage Library, 241: Alamy/Album, 243: Flickr/Biodiversity Heritage Library, 247: Flickr/Biodiversity Heritage Library.

QUOTATIONS:

Text on page 9 quoted from *The Sense of Wonder* by Rachel Carson, reproduced by kind permission of Yake Literary Management LLC for the Estate of Rachel Carson.

Text on page 57 quoted from *The Scorpio Races* by Maggie Stiefvater, reproduced by kind permission of the author.

Text on page 119 quoted from "Fireflies" by Marilyn Kallet, reproduced by kind permission of the author.

Acknowledgements

Deeply grateful. That's how I feel about all the people who have encouraged me on this writing journey.

First among them is my wife, Currie, who loves all of nature – whether a leaping dolphin, a playful otter, a fragrant gardenia, a soaring crane or an ancient redwood tree. I'm also blessed with the inspiration of children and grandchildren who often remind me of the joy, surprise and wonder in nature.

Jenny Manstead, my publisher at UniPress in London, deserves great thanks for her constant dedication to the highest quality. Meanwhile, my friend Paul Phillips has been supportive in every possible way, an immense source of strength.

In addition, I'm grateful to all the nature lovers and word lovers who gave me suggestions for this book. You were with me in spirit as I wrote each chapter. May you enjoy the reading as much as I enjoyed the writing!

Lastly, I'd like to give thanks to nature itself – to the wondrous places and living things that continue to inspire me. Especially the Maroon Bells Wilderness in my home state of Colorado, where I've often wandered on and off the trails. Like so many other areas on our beloved planet, it's a place where mystery and magic endure.

T. A. B.

First published in 2026
by Riverside Press, an imprint of
UniPress Books Ltd
World's End Studios
London SW10 0RJ
United Kingdom

Copyright in the Work © 2026 UniPress Books Ltd
Text copyright © 2026 T. A. Barron
Quotations reproduced by kind permission of the
copyright holders (see page 254)

The moral rights of the author have been asserted.

ISBN: 978-1-917226-35-6
ISBN e-book: 978-1-917226-36-3

All rights reserved.
No part of this book may be reproduced,
stored in an retrieval system or transmitted in
any form or by any means, without prior
written permission from the publisher.

This book is distributed throughout
the UK and Europe by
Abrams & Chronicle Books,
1 West Smithfield, London, EC1A 9JU
and 57 rue Gaston Tessier, 75166 Paris, France.
www.abramsandchronicle.co.uk
info@abramsandchronicle.co.uk

Commissioning Editor: Claire Collins
Design and Art Direction: Alexandre Coco
Project Manager: Katie Crous

Printed in Malaysia
riversidepress.co.uk

2 4 6 8 10 9 7 5 3 1